THE RELIGIOUS PHILOSOPHY
OF
BARON F. VON HÜGEL

THE
RELIGIOUS PHILOSOPHY
OF
BARON F. VON HÜGEL

BY

L. V. LESTER-GARLAND

(Formerly Fellow of St. John's College, Oxford)

LONDON
J. M. DENT & SONS LTD.

PREFACE

THIS little book contains the substance, and for the most part the actual text, of four public lectures which the Senate of the University of Bristol did me the honour to invite me to deliver in February and March 1932. Some of those who were present expressed the desire that they should be published. I have therefore prepared them for the press by slightly expanding some portions, and breaking them up into eight short chapters which correspond with the divisions into which the subject-matter naturally falls.

L. V. LESTER-GARLAND.

BATHFORD,
August 1932.

CONTENTS

CHAPTER I

ANY one who desires a more detailed account of the life and personal characteristics of Baron Friedrich von Hügel than is contained in the following pages will naturally turn to the Memoir by Bernard Holland which is prefixed to the edition of his *Selected Letters* which was published in 1927. Externally his life was uneventful: internally, to use his own words from the Dedication to the Memory of Dante of the First Series of *Essays and Addresses*, it meant 'some sixty years of spiritual stress'. His works are the issue, and in some degree the record, of this spiritual tension; but no attempt to elucidate the thought of one who was so singularly whole-hearted can dispense with some reference to the circumstances which surrounded him and the impressions he produced upon those who knew him.

His father, Baron Carl von Hügel, was a remarkable and many-sided man. In early youth he served in the Austrian army in the Napoleonic campaigns of 1813 and 1814. Later in life he travelled widely in almost all parts of the Old World, returned to Europe with large collections of various objects, and wrote a book

1

on Kashmir and the Sikh Kingdom. Then he entered the Austrian Diplomatic Service, and in 1850 became Austrian Minister at Florence at the Court of the Grand Duke. Here, in 1851, he married the daughter of General Francis Farquharson, whom he had met in India, and niece of Sir James Outram; and here, in 1852, Baron Friedrich was born. In 1860 Baron Carl was appointed Austrian Minister at Brussels, where the family lived for the next seven years, and where no doubt the young Friedrich must have met many interesting persons. The boy's tutor at Brussels was a Lutheran pastor. He was never at a school or university. In 1867 Baron Carl retired from the Diplomatic Service, and came to live at Torquay, where his son acquired a taste for the study of geology which he never lost in after life. He died in 1870 on a visit to Brussels. The Baroness Elizabeth, who was much younger than her husband, survived him by forty-three years, and died at Cambridge in 1913.

An attack of typhus soon after his father's death laid the foundations of a deafness from which Baron Friedrich never recovered, and which was a great trial to him all through his life. At about the same time he spent a year in Vienna and passed through a religious crisis, the issue of which he regarded as having been determined by the influence of two men. One of these was a Dutch Dominican friar, Father Raymond Hocking; the other was a French secular priest, the

Abbé Huvelin, whom he described as 'a man of vehement, seething passions and of rare forces of mind, whose will of iron, by long heroic submission to grace, had attained to a splendid tonic tenderness', and to whom he declared that he owed more than to any man he had ever known in the flesh (*Letters*, p. 5). He preserved notes of the advice given to him by the Abbé in Paris in 1886, and sometimes gave a copy of them to friends. They are printed as an appendix to the Memoir, and are of extreme interest, for they are intimate and personal in a high degree, and reflect the impression produced by von Hügel when he was thirty-four upon an exceptionally shrewd and broad-minded spiritual director.

After his father's retirement, when he was fifteen, England became his home; but he was always in touch with the Continent and frequently went abroad. At one period his winters were passed in Rome. In 1873 he married Lady Mary Herbert, daughter of Sidney Herbert, Gladstone's friend and colleague, who afterwards became Lord Herbert of Lea, and sister of the Earl of Pembroke. Three daughters were the issue of this marriage. In 1876 he took a house at Hampstead, and in 1903 he moved to 13 Vicarage Gate, Kensington, where the family remained until his death in 1925.

Von Hügel's first and longest work, *The Mystical Element of Religion*, was not published until 1908, when he was fifty-six years of age. It had grown by degrees out of what was at first intended to be a comparatively short study of St. Catharine of Genoa. Thus in this and in his subsequent books we have nothing which is not the mature result of a lifetime of profound thought and laborious study. There are no early works in which we can trace him feeling his way towards an assured philosophy of religion, or passing from one distinct phase to another. He comes into public view full-fledged, and proceeds to work out and elucidate a position already attained. Wide as is the range of subjects covered in his sixteen years of literary activity, his faith and his philosophy remained the same. There is a rock-like quality in his work which is no doubt one of the reasons of his influence in a generation in which even those who desire whole-heartedly to find a satisfying solution of the ultimate problems of life are often unable to get beyond what is tentative and provisional.

His second book, *Eternal Life*, was published in 1912. Like the *Mystical Element*, it was the result of the automatic expansion of an article which he had been asked to contribute to Hastings's *Encyclopædia of Religion and Ethics*, but proved to be far too long for the purpose. In 1916 he published *The German Soul*, a dignified protest against the unbridled denunciations of the German people and the German character as a whole which were current in some quarters at the time of the war. But he is probably best known, and his influence was most widely extended, by the two series of *Essays and Addresses on the Philosophy of Religion* which were issued, the first in 1921 and the second, after his death, in 1926. These volumes contain a number of papers on various subjects written at different dates between 1904 and 1922. We have also two invaluable volumes of his correspondence, the *Selected Letters*, 1896 *to* 1924, edited by Bernard Holland, and the *Letters from Baron von Hügel to a Niece*, Mrs. Plunket Greene. Finally, last year (1931) a posthumous work was published, entitled *The Reality of God : and Religion and Agnosticism*, containing two studies which he did not live to complete. The first, upon which he was at work up to the time of his death, seems to have been intended to be a reasoned statement of the thesis upon which his whole religious philosophy depends—the objective existence of God. The second, which was begun in 1912 and laid aside when the war broke out, never to be resumed, is a study of the character and writings of his friend Sir Alfred Lyall, the Indian administrator.

There is therefore no lack of material; but the student of von Hügel must gird up his loins. He has to do with no drawing-room philosopher, no purveyor of attractive, chatty articles for the readers of popular magazines. Philosophy and religion are for von Hügel strenuous enterprises which make the largest demands upon the mind and upon the heart, and he who embarks upon them must be prepared to pay the cost.

Moreover, his thought is closely packed, and its

sequence often obscure.   The intensity of his passion for intellectual honesty leads him to introduce qualifications of his statements and asides and parentheses which distract the attention from the point at issue and are apt to bewilder the reader.   But he never digresses without good reason, and often a seemingly casual or intrusive word or phrase suggests some unsuspected aspect of the subject under consideration which it was not his business to deal with at the time, but which he would not allow to be overlooked for the sake of clearness of statement.   'The Baron's mind,' says the Editor of the *Letters* (p. 13), 'was laborious, many-side-regarding, fully weighing, slow-moving, deeply ploughing.   He thought and wrote slowly and with difficulty, writing and rewriting and again rewriting and qualifying, because so anxious not to overstate or understate his case, and to see what could be said both for and against every position, with the aim of arriving at the most exact possible truth.'   It is not surprising to hear that three or four hours of work at the book which he had in hand was as much as he could manage in the day: the rest had to be given to being out of doors and to relaxation of the mind.   In this respect he may be compared to Charles Darwin, whose intellectual honesty and humility of mind he greatly admired.   Both men had covered a range of reading and possessed a massive wealth of learning which it might have been thought could only have been acquired by many hours of daily study; but both suffered from indifferent health and both had to be content with three or four. Darwin, we are told (*Life and Letters*, i, 113), considered that his day's work, which began at eight, was over by noon or soon after. No doubt the secret was that no time in the case of either of them was ever wasted.

He is given to the excessive use of quotations, the wealth of which is distracting to the attention. To be really effective, a quotation must be so thoroughly incorporated with the thought of the writer that it is not felt to be an intrusive element; but often this is not the case with von Hügel, and the reader finds himself wishing that he had been content to continue the statement of his argument in his own words. His work sometimes resembles what geologists call a conglomerate, in which various elements appear clamped together in some binding substance but retaining enough individuality to prevent perfect assimilation.

Again, he has a way of arguing by what may be described as the method of pistol-shots—clear-cut 'articulations' and 'discriminations' (to use phrases of his own which continually recur), numbered and ticked off with answers to correspond. This is the result of his great desire for clearness and accuracy; but it sometimes leaves the general trend of his argument disjointed and difficult to grasp as a whole. The bones of the skeleton stand out too conspicuously and seem to need a covering of flesh.

His style has been described by the Dean of St. Paul's (who nevertheless ranks him as 'one of the deepest

B

religious thinkers of our day') as 'uncouth and pon-
derous'; and no doubt there are many passages to which
this description might be applied.   His trend of thought
was Teutonic, and he was steeped in German literature.
He himself estimated, with characteristic accuracy in
the fraction, that seven-tenths of his reading had been
of German books, and it is not surprising that his
sentences sometimes exhibit a certain clumsiness and
obscurity which seem naturally attributable to his long
familiarity with continental forms and modes of
expression.

But it would be a great mistake to suppose that there
is no more to be said than this.   He often breaks out
into flashes of extreme brilliancy, sentences in which
the phrase used seems the perfect and inevitable vehicle
of the thought, concise and effective epigrams, original
and telling figures of speech.   And there are passages
in his writings which would warrant the ascription to
him of no less a title than that of a great master of
English prose.

Thus he writes of mystery in religion:

'Only through such a consciousness of reality
everywhere do we retain the feeling of mystery.   For
a sheer conundrum is not mysterious, nor is a blank
wall; but forests are mysterious, in which at first you
observe but little, yet in which, with time, you see
more and more, although never the whole; and the
starry heavens are thus mysterious, and the spirit of

man, and above all God, our origin and home' (*Reality of God*, p. 187).

Or consider the following extracts of various types:

'As well deprive a flower of its "mere details" of pistil, stamen, pollen, or an insect of its "superfluous" antennæ, as simplify any Historical Religion down to the sorry stump labelled "the religion of every honest man"' (*Essays*, i, 92).

'We have surely by now done with all this ejection and injection, with all this throwing out of a fishing tackle and drawing it back and declaring it is a fish'—speaking of theories which make religion a projection of the human mind (*Reality of God*, p. 55).

'It is by my not denying as false what I do not yet see to be true that I give myself the chance of growing in insight' (*Essays*, 1, 14).

'Philosophy no more makes religion than botany makes plants or astronomy suns and moons' (*Essays*, ii, 130).

'In actual life Natural or Rational Religion or pure Theism exists as the mirage after the setting, or as the dawn before the rising, of a Historical Religion' (*Essays*, i, xvi).

'To be hard is, indeed, to be stupid: so we will try to remain open, and will smile in welcome towards all the winds that blow in God's great heaven' (*Reality of God*, p. 30).

'Why should you, a living woman, read Locke or

Hume? Can grammar alone feed the human soul? Locke is a dreary old man; he may have a God, but he is a dusty, dim God. And Hume is blasé. He is the sort of person young people are taken in by: they take him for something else. He knows everything. He got to the bottom of everything by the time he was sixteen: he sees everything through clear glass windows. If I were to die to-night, he would know all about me by to-morrow. These old bones would be all arranged, sorted out, explained, and in his coat pocket; but somehow he would not have got me all the same' (*Letters to a Niece*, p. xiii).

A writer who can produce sentences such as these—and they could be multiplied indefinitely—reaches a very high level, not only of thought but of power of expression as well.

The upshot is that, though von Hügel's writings are continually illuminated by arresting and often unexpected flashes of extreme brilliancy, a reader must be prepared for much tough reading and much tough thought. His mind was very full both of his own thoughts and of those of other people—so full that they crowd and jostle one another, and often refuse to be reduced to orderly battalions. In this respect it is interesting to compare him with Newman, the only other religious thinker in England in recent times who can claim to be of the same importance. Newman possessed in a pre-eminent degree the power of lucid expression and of orderly arrangement, and an incomparable style.   He could convey what he thought so clearly to his hearers or readers that they had little to do but to accept what he offered them and be thankful. He could exhaust himself, as it were, for their benefit: all that there was in his mind came out and was readily accessible.   But von Hügel's writings do not exhaust his thought.   However much comes out the reader is left with the sense that there is more behind, and the instinctive desire to penetrate beneath the surface cannot be satisfied without conscious and continuous intellectual effort.   He has himself said that minds belong, roughly speaking, to two classes, (1) the mystical and positive, and (2) the scholastic and theoretical.   By this he meant that to some men thinking means the reaching out to get into touch with the world of fact and experience, infinite and for the most part unknown; to others the manipulation of systems of ideas which are definite and clearly comprehended.   Von Hügel's mind belonged to the mystical and positive type.   He distrusted clarity and he distrusted systems, because it seemed to him that as soon as the clarity is attained and the system constructed, the book is, as it were, closed, and the system divorced by the abstractive operation of the intellect from effective contact with the richness of living, concrete Reality. There is always more in life than can be contained in any system, and the one thing needful is to keep in touch with life.   Hence his writings are dynamic and suggestive, not static and theoretical.   He has no complete system of religious philosophy to present to his readers for their acceptance or rejection, but invites them to embark with him upon a great adventure, which will make demands both upon their minds and upon their hearts, but which will find its reward in a progressive approximation to the knowledge of truth: for though all the supreme realities and truths are incomprehensible they are nevertheless 'indefinitely apprehensible' (Letter to Tyrrell in *Selected Letters*, p. 71).

In spite of this detachment from systems, von Hügel's attitude and method are, in a broad sense, those of an apologist.   But the term must not be misunderstood. When the first series of the *Essays and Addresses* appeared *The Times* reviewer described him as 'the greatest living apologist for the Roman Church', to which the Baron replied in the next issue that having hoped to do well in the dog class he was much disconcerted at being given a first prize among cats.   No doubt he was a Defender of the Faith, but not of the same order as such writers as Bossuet or Lacordaire. He went deeper down, and his chief concern was the proclamation and the establishment of those facts without which any faith is impossible—the powers of the human reason, the reality of the external world, the essential goodness of creation, an ultimate superhuman Reality.   If there is not something other than the self with which the self may get into touch, Metaphysics and Religion are a mere dream.   This seemed to him a conclusion repugnant to the common sense and the almost universal instincts of mankind.

He starts with the incontrovertible fact that both in the sphere of Metaphysics and in that of Religion man is conscious of 'intimations' of Objective Reality of varying strength and depth. Men do believe in an external world, in the possibility of knowledge, in some sort of a God. The presumption is that this belief is justified. If any one says that it is illusory, the *onus probandi* lies with him. The method to be adopted by one who believes it to be true is therefore not to attempt to establish it by argument, but to rebut the arguments of those who say it is false. If the objections can be shown to be ill-founded, the belief itself is *ispo facto* established, because it does not depend upon intellectual demonstration: the vivid impression of something objective, the sense of something trans-human, stand out undimmed as soon as the fog is cleared away. It is in this sense that von Hügel is fundamentally an apologist. He attacks and destroys what he believes to be false in defence of what he believes to be true. His outlook is positive throughout. He is there to bear witness to the supreme realities, not to deliberate whether there are or are not any such things. To his sane and sturdy mind and heart Agnosticism and extreme Subjectivism were equally intolerable, and he believed that they are contrary to the common instincts of mankind.

But no one ever appreciated more fully the weight

of an opponent's arguments or gave them deeper and more conscientious consideration. Again and again he states a case against himself with such relentless power and penetration that it seems almost conclusive. He can hit very hard, as he did when he described Herbert Spencer as a flea or a bug compared to Plato, or declared that the influence of Kant has been hardly less agnostic than that of Hume himself; but there never was a more generous controversialist, or one more honest.

This book is not primarily concerned with the fervent intensity of von Hügel's own spiritual life, though it shines through all he wrote, or with his relation to that great Communion of which he always professed himself to be a loyal and devoted member. But it must always be remembered that, in the words used by Abbot Butler in an article in the *Tablet* after his death: 'Beyond all compare greater than the intellectual appeal was the moral appeal of von Hügel's personal religion'. He is so great as a thinker that this side of him is apt to be forgotten, but he cannot be understood unless it is realized that he was more than a mere thinker, and that he lived and died in the fellowship of the Roman Catholic Church.

CHAPTER II

THE METAPHYSICAL BASIS OF RELIGION.   POSITIVISM,
IDEALISM, CRITICAL REALISM

IN June 1922 von Hügel accepted the invitation of
the Senate of Edinburgh University to deliver the two
series of Gifford Lectures for the years 1924–5 and
1925–6.   The lectures were never delivered, for his
health broke down; but he continued to work at the
subject which he had chosen up to the time of his
death, and so much of the unfinished results of his
labours as were in a condition for publication have
been issued in a posthumous volume.   The title he
gave to his subject was *The Reality of God*; but he
appended to the first part a sub-title more particularly
defining his scope—'Concerning the Reality of Finites
and the Reality of God: a Study of their Inter-relations
and their Effects and Requirements within the Human
Mind'.   It is probably safe to assume that his intention
was to bind together into a reasoned whole the various
strands of thought which are to be found scattered
through his writings.   However that may be, there
can be no doubt that the idea of Reality, as he understood it, is the foundation upon which the whole of his
religious philosophy is built.

15

By that which is *real* he meant something which has an objective existence independent of the mind of the thinking subject. The external world, the finite personalities of other human beings, the Supreme Reality which is God Himself stand out as distinct from and other than the mind which apprehends them. Men can, and do, spin systems of Metaphysics and Philosophies of Religion out of their own thoughts and their own emotions; but in so far as these have a merely subjective origin, though they may lead to something which has a sort of shadowy existence in the world of abstractions, there is no sort of security that they correspond to any world of concrete existence. But the mind and the soul live by contact with what is external to them, by looking outwards and upwards: self-imprisonment means degeneration, and ultimately death. Religion cannot be resolved into a succession of inward spiritual experiences: it is based upon the recognition of, and grows by communication with, Something which owes no part of its reality to any subjective activity of the religious consciousness.

If everything depends upon this belief, it is vital that it should be shown to be capable of defence against any one who chooses to assert either that there is no such thing as Objective Reality, or that if there is it is impossible for man to attain to any knowledge of it. The attack may be met in two ways. Either an attempt may be made to demonstrate *a priori* that the objectively real must exist; or, if it is found that such a logical demonstration can never carry complete conviction in dealing with a subject of this nature, it must be shown that the universal presumption that Reality does exist and is in a true sense knowable is rationally justifiable and makes the best sense of the universe.

Now von Hügel nowhere makes any attempt to prove the fact of the existence of God by deductive reasoning, for the simple reason that arguments of this kind, in his opinion, never get into touch with Reality at all. He draws a clear-cut distinction between two kinds of knowledge, one of which deals with abstract ideas and the other with concrete facts. A series of deductions may be clear, consistent, and logically irrefragable, but it nowhere involves the affirmation of particular, concrete existences. The science of mathematics, for instance, does not assert that such things as straight lines and circles and triangles exist, but that, if they exist, they possess certain properties and that there are certain relations between them. But the point at issue is not whether, if there is a God, we can deduce by logic what His properties and attributes must be, but whether He exists at all. There is something deeper here than the question of the consistency between the various links in a chain of reasoning: we are concerned with the nature of the first link, on which the whole chain depends; and this is a matter which cannot be approached by the same method which led to the formation of the chain. The question of existence or non-existence, which the deductive method leaves in the air, is precisely the question which clamours for an answer. We have passed out of the realm of logic and clear-cut ideas, and want to know whether there is, or is not, behind it another realm of concrete fact which supplies an unconditioned and positive basis to which a chain of reasoning may be attached.

If there is such a realm of objective existence, the knowledge of it will be different from the knowledge of the relations between abstract ideas. The implications of a fact are inexhaustible. It has relations with nothing less than the sum total of all other facts. To know completely the meaning of any one fact would involve the knowledge of the whole of creation. Such knowledge of facts as we can attain is therefore very different from the clear-cut conceptions which we can form of abstract ideas and their relations. In that case we are dealing with something definite, limited, as it were, closed: in this the only thing to do is to keep the mind open. There is no way to the knowledge of facts but by the interpretation of experience: for the possibilities of experience are unlimited, and our own experience always contains far more than we have formulated or systematized; and instead of concerning ourselves with questions of consistency within self-imposed limits we start upon a voyage of discovery into the territory of the unknown.

It is with facts, according to von Hügel, that Religion has to deal. It is not merely an interior life of the soul, but a reaching out to something which is other than itself. If there is no such thing as trans-human Reality or if it is inaccessible to human apprehension, there is no such thing as Religion in his sense of the word. 'The thirst for Religion,' he says, 'is at bottom a metaphysical thirst, and the intimations of Religion are, ultimately, metaphysical intimations' (*Essays*, ii, 207). Consequently, the first thing necessary is a theory of knowledge which will explain how man gets into touch both with the Reality manifested in the external world and with the Supreme Reality which lies behind it.

He never writes as if he himself possessed or knew exactly where to find such a theory in a complete and perfect form. It is something to be fervently desired and patiently worked out. Thus he says in a letter to Professor M. Guiran of Lausanne, dated 11 July 1921:

'Je dois avouer que mon intérêt pleinement vivant est maintenant donné aux penseurs — à peu près tous Allemandes, Anglais et Italiens — qui sont en train de nous constituer une épistémologie critico-réaliste' (*Letters*, p. 333).

But he is in no doubt about the general characteristics of a theory such as he desired, and he leaves us in no doubt about the name. In the Preface to *Eternal Life* (quoted *Letters*, p. 37) he says:

'A Critical Realism, a Realism not of Categories or Ideas, but of Organisms and Spirits, of *the* Spirit, a purified but firm Anthropomorphism, are here maintained throughout as essential to the full vigour and clear articulation of Religion.'

And in the Preface to the second edition of *The Mystical Element in Religion* (p. xvi) he writes:

'The central and final philosophic system and temper of mind which is alone genuinely appropriate to the subject-matter of Religion is, I cannot doubt, some kind of Realism—not a Naïve Realism (which would simply ignore all the mixture of truth and error since Descartes and the criticism also of Kant's first Critique itself), but a *Critical Realism*, constituted after the most careful sifting of these various Idealisms, Materialisms, even Scepticisms—theories which often bear along, in their muddy or perverse currents, fragments of truth demanding incorporation in a system truly congenial to them.' And he goes on to describe himself as growing 'more and more attached to that current of Realism which finds its first and still largely unsurpassed exponent in Plato, and in modern times is represented by Thomas Reid and then by those late and more or less intermittent, astonishingly vivid insights of Kant'.

In the essay on 'The Specific Genius of Christianity' he gives a condensed summary of his idea of a Critical Realism:

'Everywhere such a Realism would assume or announce that thought, primarily and normally, never stands alone, and never is thought of thought, but always thought of a reality distinct from this thinking of it; that the activity of the human mind and soul, as known to us in this life, always more or less requires sense-stimulation, and that superstition here lies as truly in denying as in exaggerating this need; that our knowledge is always an incomplete knowledge, yet a knowledge of reality—since the objects really reveal in various degrees their real nature; that the primary qualities of material objects are trans-subjectively real, and that the instinctive recognition of this reality plays an important part also in the religious habits and certainties of the soul; that the mystical type of religion is indeed secondary and reflective in so far as it seeks and sees *all things* as immediately present, but that the original religious fact and experience of religion already always contains an *element* of immediacy' (*Essays*, i, 189).

Now the solutions which have been proposed of the fundamental problem of Metaphysics may be said roughly to belong to three types: (1) Scepticism, with its variety Positivism; (2) Idealism; (3) Realism; and we shall get further light upon his own position by contrasting it with his treatment of the other two. On Scepticism pure and simple he does not waste much powder. He regarded it as a *reductio ad absurdum*, an extravagance which destroys itself by its own excess, which may be left ultimately to the common sense of mankind. Moreover, he thought that the twentieth century has seen 'a marked retrocession', at all events for a time, of Materialism and Agnosticism, and that the danger at present lies elsewhere (*Essays*, ii, 137). His real foes are Positivism and Subjective Idealism.

In *The Mystical Element of Religion* (ii, 275 ff.) he devotes a section to the consideration of 'Mysticism and the limits of human knowledge and experience', in which he attacks the Epistemology of Positivism. The argument is extremely condensed, and the copious use of quotations from other thinkers, especially from the German philosopher Volkelt, does not make it easier to follow; but it is important because it does contain something like a formal statement of his own metaphysical position.

He begins with roundly characterizing the Positivist limitation of trans-subjectively valid knowledge to direct sense-perception and to the laws of the so-called empirical experiences as 'a mere vulgar error'; and he does so on these grounds.

(1) The only absolutely indisputable fact is the bare occurrence of our sensations and impressions. These are sometimes accompanied by 'a pressure upon our minds to credit them with trans-subjective validity'. This pressure is itself an undeniable part of our experience, which, however, theoretically might be merely misleading. But no one has ever yet succeeded in consistently carrying through a refusal of assent to its truth, because scepticism derives the very weapons which it uses against the trans-subjectivity of this impression from the acceptance of other impressions

which exert the same 'pressure' as trans-subjectively valid. It is therefore self-destructive. The fact is that logical cognition, which every one (including the sceptic) practises, goes beyond what the Positivist means by 'immediate experience' at every step. The immediately experienced presentations already in themselves constitute a knowledge, and 'the entire range of Reality, down to its last depths, lies open to cognition'. This knowledge is real and not illusory; but since we do not come to see objective Reality simply face to face, it is possible for the mind to resist the pressure which urges it on towards the belief in the objective, and 'an act of endorsement, a kind of faith is necessary on its part'. The possibility of knowledge therefore seems ultimately to rest upon what he elsewhere calls 'the rational presumption that the spontaneous and universal testimony of our minds (after deduction of such points or forms as can be clearly shown to be merely subjective) is truly indicative of the several trans-subjective realities which these experiences so obstinately proclaim' (*Essays*, i, 51). The position of Kant—that we can know nothing about trans-subjective reality, but that it is quite different from what our experience seems to indicate it to be—'can doubtless not be maintained as reasonable', he says, 'by any mind once vividly aware of the inconsistency'. The sceptic himself, if he is to be effective, must practise this trust (*Essays*, i, 69). Thus the cognitive process is not simple, but at the very source of all our certainty we find three elements:

C

'indubitable sensation, clear thought, warm faith in and through action' (*Mystical Element*, i, 57).

(2) The acquisition of even the most rudimentary knowledge involves both an emotional disposition and volitional action.   It is the whole man and not the mind only that is active.   Pure, isolated thought, which is sometimes set up as an ideal, is in real life more or less of a fiction—something shadowy and insignificant.   'Even receptivity,' in the words of Professor Ward, 'is activity'; and the deeper and richer the subject-matter with which the thinker is dealing, the stronger and more prominent is the emotional and volitional note.   From this it would seem to follow that for von Hügel the part played by the intellect in the apprehension of the Ultimate Reality is secondary to the parts played by the emotions and the will, and that if that Reality is the true counterpart of man's subjective activity it must be something 'possessed of a positive aim and alive according to the analogy of a willing individual.   The world would thus be a logical process,' to quote James Ward again, 'only in the sense that this concrete, fundamental Power is bound by the ideal necessity of its own nature'.

(3) However important the intellectual distinction between the objective and the subjective may be, it must not be pressed so far as to imply a metaphysical exclusion of the one by the other.   There is no fundamental dualism.   'Pure thought and the manifold of sense,' in Professor Henry Jones's words, 'pass

into each other.' They are only aspects of one fact. 'Intelligence is never purely formal, and the material with which it deals is nowhere a pure manifold.' If we could begin with the purely subjective we should no doubt end there; but 'the purely subjective is as completely beyond our reach as the purely objective'. This amounts to saying that all experience and all knowledge are syntheses, the difference between them being that in experience the contact with the objective factor is direct, while in knowledge it is attained indirectly through reflection.

(4) A further illustration of the interaction of contingent fact and logical necessity is afforded by the observed relation between history and philosophy. Historic forces do not appear at first sight to follow the laws of logical development; yet the introduction of religious, political, artistic, and other motives is found not to confuse or spoil philosophical thinking but actually to advance it. This is only explicable by supposing 'the operative presence of some original, teleological inter-relation', some pre-existing harmony, which binds all these activities together into a whole, so that each, while consciously pursuing its own laws and standards, in reality furthers the objects of all the rest. This argument he borrows from Volkelt.

(5) That of which we have the most direct and adequate experience is not, as it might at first sight appear, the world of things, but the world of mind and will. This follows from the fact that the only experience

immediately accessible to us is our own. We are farther off, in a sense, from the adequate apprehension of a pebble or a plant or a star than from the apprehension of God Himself, because in the contemplation of the purely contingent, the simply phenomenal and finite, we are conscious of 'a sense of mental oppression, of intolerable imprisonment'. The higher the grade of Reality which is under contemplation, the more satisfying and the more certain does our experience become; and those whom the testimony of mankind has ranked among its greatest souls have felt most strongly the unconquerable urge which makes it impossible for them to rest anywhere short of the highest.

To sum up, we may say that, so far from the Positivist circumscription of knowledge being admissible, all kinds of experience at all stages involve the elements which the Positivist rejects, and that the most certain and adequate knowledge is precisely that of which he denies the very existence.

We have next to consider his attitude towards Idealism. Now all Theists, in the ordinary meaning of the word, must repudiate scepticism. If there is nothing behind phenomena, there is no God: if knowledge of what is behind phenomena is impossible, you are not much better off. But among convinced and sincere Theists there have been many in each of the opposing camps of Idealism and Realism. Thus we find the late Dr. Rashdall roundly asserting that 'Idealism is the necessary basis of Theism for minds which want to get to the bottom of things' (*Contentio Veritatis*, p. 8), while von Hügel is equally certain that Religion must be founded upon Realism.   The gulf between them is not as deep as it seems.   Idealism is an ambiguous word, and Rashdall was contrasting it with Materialism, while von Hügel was thinking of the contrast between his own conception of Religion, the very essence of which is the recognition of an Objective Reality, with the extreme subjectivism of some representatives of the Idealist school.   But the fact remains that among Theists there are two schools of thought, which approach the study of the philosophy of Religion from different points of view, and lay the chief emphasis on different elements of the problem.

Modern Idealist Philosophy is, in his view, the off-spring of an intense desire to make sure of that interior sincerity which must be the condition of any honest attempt to attain to knowledge.   Descartes, its founder, in his famous formula *Cogito, ergo sum*, thought that he had brought what is absolutely certain down to an irreducible minimum.   But this very eagerness led its adherents into an initial error which vitiated their conclusions.   They started 'not from the concrete fact, viz. a mind thinking *something* and from the analysis of this ultimate trinity in unity (the subject, the thinking, and the object), but from that pure abstraction —thinking or thought or a thinking of a thought' (*Essays*, i, 186).   This von Hügel calls an 'unreal starting-point', because 'Man's actual experiences, the data with which he starts, are never simply impressions which are felt by man at the time of his receiving them as purely subjective', nor can they be shown to be merely subjective by philosophical analysis (*Essays*, i, 51). The single human consciousness includes both subject and object, 'each giving to and taking from the other'. Starting from Idealist premises—that is to say, setting out in search of a problematical object from the purely subjective—Hume had no difficulty in arriving at the purest scepticism.

The influence of Kant, though his intention was to establish Theism upon unshakable foundations, 'has been, upon the whole, hardly less agnostic than that of Hume himself' (*Essays*, i, 186). For apart altogether from the question of his contribution to Ethics, his theory of knowledge, stated broadly, comes to this, that man really knows nothing of the real nature of anything, though he does know that the reality of everything is quite different from what the thing appears to be. Here is a self-contradiction which von Hügel says 'can doubtless not be maintained as reasonable by any mind once vividly aware of the inconsistency'. It is true that we 'cannot get clean out of our mind, so as to compare things as they are outside it with the same things as we experience them within it'; but 'we have every solid reason for, and no cogent reason against' holding that what we persistently apprehend as real *is* real and is 'not all unlike to, not disconnected with, what we apprehend it to be'.

As a typical representative of the extreme sub-jectivist position he takes the German philosopher Feuerbach, not in his last phase when he became a sheer materialist but in the earlier period when he was still dominated by the influence of Hegel. Note the motive underlying the selection. Feuerbach is chosen as the ablest exponent of this school of thought, and as beyond the reach of possible personal reactions which might affect the living; and he is taken when he is at his best and strongest. Feuerbach's position is that man essentially consists of mind alone: that the human mind can penetrate or be penetrated by nothing but itself: that it never gains any real knowledge of any reality other than man himself—not merely of the individual man, but of man as a species. 'There is thus, from first to last, in human experience only one object—the subject itself, illusively mistaken,' accord-ing to Feuerbach, 'for something different from this subject; and true philosophy consists in unmasking this inevitable, persistent illusion' (*Essays*, i, 32).

Von Hügel's reply is that this reading of the meta-physical position leaves out half the facts. Life, history, science all prove it to be inadequate. 'Man is not simply mind, but also sense, imagination, feeling, will.' 'The mind itself is not simply abstractive or discursive, but intuitive as well.' The human personality holds all these elements together, and they are developed and built up into a whole only by contact with other minds, other living beings, other things. Of all these man achieves some real knowledge, and through his relations with them he attains some real knowledge of himself. He is always 'in the first instance necessarily related not to an idea or representation either of himself or of anything else but to various concrete realities, distinct from, though not entirely unlike, himself'. Thus the action of this objective world upon him, and his reaction to it are primary: the abstracting activity is 'secondary and instrumental', and lags far behind these primary activities.

This amounts to a robust assertion of the truth of what may be called the common-sense view clarified by its passage through a philosophic mind. No ordinary person doubts, except perhaps in abnormal moments, that there is an objective world which is distinct from himself, or that he is in touch with it. All his activities of mind and body are based upon this postulate. That men do act upon this belief is undeniable: the fact that the belief is practically universal affords a strong presumption that it is well-founded. Von Hügel does not scruple again and again to use the argument that human reason and human instincts are upon the whole to be depended upon. He has a strong faith in both. If neither can be trusted in this respect, there is an end of both metaphysics and religion. This seemed to him a preposterous conclusion, with which the sense of mankind will never be satisfied. The man in the street is right, so far as he goes, and his convictions constitute a court of appeal to which philosophy may have recourse for its justification.

He deals with the Idealist conception of the Absolute on similar lines. The Absolute, in theories of this type, in spite of the infinite variety of its manifestations in the phenomenal world or in the minds of men, is a single circumscribed whole, complete in itself, with nothing outside it. It is therefore a sort of closed system, comparable to the Nature of the materialist philosophy of the nineteenth century, with mind substituted for matter. In spite of unceasing kaleidoscopic internal rearrangements there is nothing really new, no 'creativity', to use a modern term. We thus get a static Universe. There is a concrete unity of thought which lies behind the thoughts of individual men, in terms of which alone they become intelligible, but it remains a unity which is complete and can never become more than it is.

Now the Realist raises the question whether the Idealist has got to the bottom of the matter. Is the Absolute in the Hegelian sense really ultimate? Is there nothing behind it? It is clearly an advance upon the barren Unity of the Eleatic School of Philosophy among the Greeks which was altogether devoid of content, because it provides for multiplicity in unity. But is it less of an abstraction? Von Hügel's answer was in the negative. There must be something behind the Universe regarded as a whole. He protests against 'the persuasion that the whole of the Absolute—that

God in and for Himself—has been and is absorbed in
God as Creator' (*Essays*, ii, 206).   That is the straight
road to Pantheism.   'Hegel,' he says, 'is an uncom-
fortable ally for Christianity; Christian though he
certainly intended to be and thought himself, Pantheist
is what his philosophy incurably persists in being'
(*Essays*, ii, 173).   The Ultimate Reality must be
transcendent—immanent also, of course, in some sense,
but something other than and independent of the
Universe.   We have seen how intimate von Hügel
believed the connection between metaphysics and
religion to be.   To him the essence of religion is
that it deals with the transcendent, as he understood
it, and a metaphysic which stops short of transcendence
fails at the critical point.   Hence he finds all Hegelian
interpretations of religion unsatisfying and unfruitful,
and much as he admired some of the writers belonging
to the English Idealist school, especially Thomas Hill
Green and Edward Caird, he became more and more
convinced of the inadequacy of their treatment of
religion.

To sum up von Hügel's position, which is essentially
the same in Metaphysics and Religion, we may say:

(1) That he is convinced that the datum of all the
sciences is something which has an objective existence
independent of the perceiving mind, and that the datum
of religion, that is, the Ultimate Reality, is equally
independent of the mind of the religious man.

(2) That in Science and in Religion the datum is

not merely an inert object of contemplation, but the focus of an activity which affects and communicates with the contemplator. The mind and spirit of man receive what is presented to them; but they on their side are not mere passive recipients: they also contribute an activity which fuses with the activity of the Object, so that both Knowledge and Religion are of the nature of a synthesis. There is a movement from within outwards, as well as a movement from without inwards (*Mystical Element*, ii, 388).

(3) The objective existence of what is real and the possibility of knowledge of it are not matters which are demonstrable by pure ratiocination. Their proof rests ultimately upon a trust or faith of which even the sceptical philosopher is bound to avail himself when he attacks them. If reason cannot prove by deduction that knowledge is possible, it is equally incapable of proving that it is impossible, for the only weapon the sceptic can use is just that the existence of which he is seeking to deny.

CHAPTER III

IF it is held that Metaphysics justify the universal belief in an Objective Reality and in the possibility of the knowledge of it, the way lies open to the consideration of its nature.

A preliminary question of vital importance presents itself at the outset. Aristotle long ago thought it worth while to observe that it is irrational to expect greater clearness than the nature of the subject under consideration permits. This sounds like a truism; but the neglect of what is obviously true has often been the prolific source of error and confusion. What kind or degree of clearness may we expect in our knowledge of Reality, and especially in our knowledge of the Supreme Reality? To enter upon the study of Religion without the realization of what is possible and what is not possible, without the right temper of mind, or at least an honest desire for the right temper, is, in von Hügel's words, waste of time or worse, 'because we are then certain to come away more rebellious and empty, or more despairing and bitter, or considerably more sceptical' than we were to begin with (*Essays*, i, 105).

34

He draws a distinction, as we have seen, between two kinds of apprehension. There is the knowledge of abstract ideas and numerical and spatial relations. This knowledge is clear, undeniable, and readily transferable from one mind to another, because it does not directly involve any affirmation of particular, concrete existences or realities. It is all within the mind, and amenable to the mind's operations. We can have abstract ideas, for instance, of largeness or smallness, or can build up whole systems of mathematical relations without implying that such things exist. But the case is different when you come to 'affirmations of real existences and of real qualities attaching to such existences' (*Essays*, i, 101). Then the mind is no longer dealing with clear-cut conceptions, with fragmentary aspects of things to which it can confine itself and which it can manipulate at pleasure: it is hitched to Reality, plunged at once into unknown depths. Knowledge loses its simplicity and transparency and embarks upon an uncharted ocean.

Moreover, the higher the grade of reality with which any kind of knowledge is concerned, the more complicated and difficult does that knowledge become. There is more to know in a daisy than in a rock crystal, in a dog than in a daisy, in a man than in a dog. The difficulty of adequate knowledge increases with what he calls the 'richness' of the reality, and in the case of the Supreme Reality it becomes supreme. Von Hügel does not scruple to use such an expression as 'our

confusedly concrete sense of the infinite'.   He is not
the least afraid of it; quite the contrary.   'If I could
understand religion,' he says in *Letters to a Niece*
(p. xvii), 'as I understand that two and two make
four, it would not be worth understanding.   Religion
can't be clear if it is worth having.   To me, if I can
see things through and through, I get uneasy—I feel
it 's a fake.   I know I have left something out, I 've
made some mistake.'   This is another way of express-
ing the same truth which underlies his contention,
referred to in the last chapter, that we can know God
better than we know a pebble or a star.   That is true
because the knowledge of a pebble leaves our higher
aspirations unsatisfied: in the same way it is true that
the very clearness and limitation of our knowledge of
abstractions is inadequate for the comprehension of
rich, concrete Reality.

Now it is of course possible to deal with Reality,
even with the Supreme Reality, by the method of
abstraction.   We can take isolated aspects and characteristics of which we can form clear ideas and combine
them into a more or less coherent system.   This is
what philosophy does, and different philosophical
systems do undoubtedly provide pictures of the universe
which are definite and as clearly apprehensible as
mathematical systems.   Abstract philosophical ideas are
not necessarily obscure or confused.   On the other
hand, von Hügel often asserts that all philosophies and
all religions, even those with which he was himself in

least sympathy, contain elements of real value, so far as they go. They fail, not because they are entirely false, but because they are inadequate and partial in so far as they go.

The crucial fact is that we get our knowledge of what exists from experience, and that our experience contains far more than we are consciously aware of when we receive it, or than we can reduce to a system by subsequent reflection. This is true of all grades of experience, but the higher the grade, the richer and fuller is the content. Experience is the action of the objective world upon the human subject; and the manifold reaction of the human subject to the world's action, and the more real the object which stimulates and the subject who is stimulated, the richer will be the stimulation and the response (*Essays*, i, 33). The response to the stimulation of the Ultimate Reality will therefore be, not a simple matter susceptible of a clear-cut, easily intelligible formulation, but as wide and as deep as the whole nature of the stimulated subject; and beyond the range of any individual finite mind there is the whole sketch of the infinite waiting, as it were, to be apprehended, as far as may be. 'All the supreme realities and truths, supremely deserving and claiming our assent and practice,' he says in a letter to Tyrrell, 'are both *incomprehensible* and *indefinitely apprehensible*, and the constant vivid realization of these two qualities inseparably inherent to all our knowledge and practice of them, is of primary and equal importance to us'

(*Letters*, p. 71). Supreme Realities are 'indefinitely apprehensible'—this is the keynote of his approach to philosophy and religion. Both, to him, are mere dead systems of abstract ideas unless they are in touch with what *is*, and continually drawing accessions of life from the depths of an unfathomed and unfathomable ocean of Being, which is nevertheless 'indefinitely apprehensible'. The religious philosopher should 'see all truth as a centre of intense light losing itself gradually in utter darkness: this centre would gradually extend, but the borders would ever remain fringe, they could never become clear-cut lines' (Preface to *Readings in von Hügel*, p. xii).

Is it the case then that mankind, where a clear knowledge would seem to be of the utmost importance for life and action, must be content with one that is 'confused' and 'obscure'? Von Hügel's reply is that when you are dealing with existences intellectual clarity is not everything. 'I take it,' he writes to Miss Petre (*Letters*, p. 90), 'that we must remember how all our conceptions can be rendered fully clear only by means of images derived from and projected into space; and all such images are static and quantitative. Whereas when we come to the natures of the strictly spiritual and moral being and life, we are in the midst of the *dynamic* and *qualitative*, hence of what we can conceive only either truly and then with a conscious vagueness, or clearly and then with an unconscious obliteration or falsification of all its true characteristics. Better far will it be to choose the former alternative.' And in the Letter to a Bereaved Lady on the Preliminaries of Religious Belief, he distinguishes the proper tests for the adequacy of each kind of knowledge. 'The affirmations which concern abstractions and spatial, numerical, mechanical relations,' he says, 'may be ever so empty and conditional; if they are clear and readily transferable, they are appropriate and adequate. The affirmations which concern existences and realities may be ever so dim and difficult to transmit; if they are rich and fruitful, they are appropriate and true' (*Essays*, i, 105).

Thus the one thing needful for this kind of knowledge is not clarity, but suggestiveness. It must be 'vivid' and 'fruitful'. It must not conduct the thinker inside a ring-fence and leave him there, but bring him into touch with all the various forms and grades of reality which surround him. To expect clearness, von Hügel says with rather startling vehemence, 'indicates a thoroughly unreasonable, a self-contradictory habit of mind' (*Essays*, i, 100). The doors and windows of the mind must be left open, and he is suspicious of any kind of barrier such as a formulated system may easily provide. He was content to leave many questions undecided: he enters a caveat against 'too great tidying up': he writes in the Preface to the first series of *Essays and Addresses*: 'There is assuredly not a paper here which does not raise more problems than it solves'. Even in his monumental structures of

D

thought, such as the *Mystical Element* or the elaborate but unfinished essay upon *The Reality of God*, on which he was engaged at the time of his death, he is more concerned with breaking up the soil than with trimming the lawns.   He is always a pioneer.

Bearing in mind this important preliminary distinction between the two kinds of knowledge, we may proceed to consider von Hügel's attitude towards the various theories which have been propounded of the nature of the Supreme Reality.   These theories fall into two classes according as they assert or deny the attribute of Personality.   All other differences are unimportant in comparison with this.   The choice lies between some form of Theism with a Personal God or Gods, and the acceptance of some supposedly all-pervasive abstraction as ultimate.   Such abstractions are popular nowadays, for men 'have suffered much at the hands of theologians' (*Essays*, ii, 123) and there is a violent reaction.   Moreover, the scientific temper demands clearness above all things.   But to all such theories he would deny the name of religion.   A religion without a Personal God is to him 'the strangest of truncations and abstractions' (*Essays*, ii, 122).   In an address delivered at Oxford in 1920 he said:

'I take the restriction of Religion to belief (whatever may be its other qualities or its quantity) in some Superhuman Beings or Being to be the most adequate interpretation of the great mass of historical and psychological facts and forces concerning religion, so long as we carefully distinguish these facts and forces from the fancies or wishes, or from the difficulties and scepticisms of individuals or of times that have been deflected or arrested, in their naïve religious instincts, by over-civilization or the like' (*Essays*, ii, 157).

He admits that Theism is not free from 'very real theoretical difficulties and practical dangers', and is sensible of the superficial attractiveness of the attempt to resolve religion, as it has flourished in history and as it still subsists among average human beings, into 'a vague religiosity, fearful of any approach to anthropomorphism however noble'. But any such attempted reduction is bound to fail, because it does not account for the fact that wherever religion has existed it has always meant the sense of 'the Otherness, the Distinct Reality, the Personalism of God'. He will not allow that Buddhism or Confucianism, the two most important apparent exceptions, are religions at all, in his sense of the word. Primitive Buddhism was rather 'a grand prelude, an impressive clearing of the stage', than a religion, and modern Buddhism is 'admittedly penetrated by belief in supernatural beings'; while Confucianism is no more than 'an impressively definite, and within its range an extraordinarily efficient, moral code' (*Essays*, ii, 158).

Theism has been attacked on two grounds. It has been urged:

(1) That the idea of Personality implies limitation, and that the Infinite cannot be limited.

(2) That Theism is based upon anthropomorphism. Man simply makes a God in his own image, who is no more than a projection upon the void of human nature on a vaster scale.

(1) In *The Idea of God* (p. 294) Dr. Pringle Pattison asks: 'How can we ascribe to the Absolute the self-centred life which spells moral death in the creature?' The most effective reply to this question is an appeal to the conception of the freedom of God which was formulated by Augustine and elaborated by Aquinas (*Essays*, ii, 220). It is true that God must be free: it is also true that He alone is perfectly free. Man possesses an imperfect kind of freedom, the chief characteristic of which appears to him to be that he has the power of choice: hence he is apt to think that the freedom of God consists in an *unlimited* power of choice, as he is apt to think of eternity as unlimited time. But he is wrong. The characteristic of perfect freedom is that it *excludes* choice (*Essays*, ii, 202). Augustine said: 'It is already a great freedom to be able not to sin. But the greatest freedom consists in the inability to sin'. Extend the application of this principle and you reach the apparently paradoxical conclusion that a thing becomes more perfect the more rigidly it is limited, until in the case of what is absolutely perfect the limitation becomes complete, as it is often said of a great work of art that any alteration of the least kind would spoil it. What then is the difference

between the principle of limitation which pervades all created things and the same principle as manifested in the activities of the Creative Power? It consists in this, that the limitation in the first case is imposed from outside, while in the second case it is the spontaneous expression of a perfect nature. Therefore to the argument that God cannot be a Person because Personality implies limitation while God is infinite, the answer is that it depends upon what you mean by limitation. Von Hügel's conclusion is:

'That we can safely hold with Lotze, not only that Personality is compatible with Infinitude, but that the personality of all finite beings can be shown to be imperfect precisely because of their Finitude," and hence that 'Perfect Personality is compatible only with the conception of an Infinite Being; finite beings can only achieve an approximation to it' (*Essays*, i, 50).

(2) And with regard to the objection that Theism is anthropomorphic, with the implied corollary that on that account it cannot conduct man into the transcendental presence of the Infinite, Feuerbach argued that if the attributes usually ascribed to God—love, wisdom, goodness, personality (the reality and value of which he did not deny)—are human attributes, the belief in a God is an anthropomorphism too, a presupposition purely human. And he went on to argue not, as might have been expected, that *if* these attributes are real there seems to be no obvious reason why such a belief should not be equally real, but that *because* they

are real they need no such belief to support them. The idea of God is dependent on the idea of justice, goodness, wisdom, etc.; but the converse does not hold' (*Essays*, i, 38). Thus man can get all he wants for the conduct of life without postulating the existence of an objective Divine Being.

Von Hügel's answer to this is that it is obviously true that 'everything that is apprehended by any apprehending being is apprehended according to the manner of this being's apprehension', quoting from Aquinas. Man can never jump out of his own skin. Even the God of the Hebrews 'appears as anthropopathic, as possessed of thoroughly human psychic emotions' (*Essays*, ii, 183). Yet it is certain that man does possess 'a more or less continuous, often most painful, sense of the inadequacy of any and all merely human mode and degree of existence and of apprehension' (*Essays*, i, 40). This sense is too fundamental, too closely bound up with all his noblest achievements in science, philosophy, art, ethics, life generally, to be dismissed as a sheer delusion, or (what comes to much the same thing) to be resolved into a mere race-instinct. The only explanation of this dissatisfaction with everything human, felt to be imperfect, is to admit the existence of a perfect Reality 'sufficiently like us to be able to penetrate and to move us through and through' —immanent, as it could not be if it were wholly unlike, transcendent, as it could not be if it were wholly like. This means that the fact that it is anthropomorphic is no objection to Theism: it could not be anything else. It would be a fatal objection if it could be proved that it is *solely* anthropomorphic, that there was nothing in man's nature which pointed to or implied anything beyond or unlike itself; but this supposition is definitely negatived, to a stalwart realist like von Hügel, by the evidence supplied by the analysis of man's activities in every sphere. There is 'a natural conformity between God and rational creatures' (*Mystical Element*, i, 261); but this is not because man has made God in his own image, but because God has made man in His.

In his address to the Anglican Fellowship on 'The Idea of God', delivered at Oxford in 1918, he asks: 'What are the great rival systems with which Theism has to contend?' Note that he does not treat them as pure negations of the truth. He regards them as 'tendencies which in varying degrees, ways, and combinations obstruct or obscure, deflect or distort' it. Each represents 'an over-emphasis, or mistaken extension, or misinterpretation, always plausible and mostly nearly true, of certain great facts or laws and of certain moods or cravings present in the wide, rich, and complex world around us and in the many-levelled soul-life within us' (*Essays*, ii, 136). The currents may be muddy and turbid, but they carry truth along with them none the less. These rival systems he takes to be four.

(1) Materialism, which he calls 'always by far the clearest and simplest, apparently the most certain of all possible outlooks', with its intense sense of the reality of the external world and of our own bodies, and only a shadowy, evanescent realization of the world of mind, soul, spirit, character, personality.

(2) Pluralism, 'next in degree of clearness, which holds the Ultimate Reality to consist of at least two distinct substances, or wills, or persons, each limiting the others, and each essentially finite in nature and capacity'.

(3) Pantheism, 'with its thirst for Oneness and for the Whole and its tendency to resolve all things into more or less transitory appearances or parts of a single Reality, an Absolute which is itself free from all spatial or temporal, indeed from all ethical and spiritual, determinations whatever'.

(4) Agnosticism, which rests upon the obvious facts of 'the manifold limitations and infirmities of the human mind, and of the inexhaustibleness of the realities which still baffle as they confront us'.

It is against Pantheism that von Hügel directs his heaviest artillery. The Materialism and Agnosticism which loomed so large in the last half of the nineteenth century he considered, as we have seen, to have fallen into the background. And with the philosophical system of Pantheism he constantly connects the temper of mind known as Subjectivism. Not that they are logically related: they are really incompatible, because

Subjectivism, he says, 'if pressed, would make short work of the God of Pantheism'; but they are often found together and he treats them as allied foes.　Thus, 'If we look at the more characteristically modern movements and attitudes around us concerning the inner life,' he writes, 'we shall I think find that they are, conciously or unconsciously, full of Pantheism and Subjectivism' (*Essays*, ii, 119).　Both are equally fatal to his deepest convictions.　If the Ultimate Reality is a totality and nothing more, there is no room for a Personal God: if man can never get beyond his own senses, feelings, imagination, mind, he can have no use for an Objective Reality, even if it exists.　He repudiates both on the same grounds, that they leave out the most important facts and consequently can never permanently satisfy.

Against Pantheism he argues as follows:

(*a*) The comparative study of religions shows that animistic and other earlier forms have given way to personalistic conceptions which find God to be distinct from Nature, however true it may be that Nature has come from Him and is penetrated by Him.　Whatever difficulties the presence of evil in the world may put in the way of belief in an all-good, all-powerful God, at all events we do not worship that world, 'nor,' he says, 'will superstitious scientists ever succeed in popularizing such a double-dyed unreality of mind' (*Essays*, ii, 120).

(*b*) The analysis of man's metaphysical and religious experience points to the existence of something other than, and of a different order to, the phenomenal. Thus we have an abstract conception of Time, by which we measure the sequence of events in the world; but we *live* not in abstract Time but in concrete Time or 'Duration', the elements of which are not purely successive but partly simultaneous, and this leads on to the idea of the perfectly simultaneous, the eternal. Again, we possess an obstinate conviction of the reality of the external world and its appearances which extends even to the secondary qualities of things—'to the particular tone and inflection of my brother's voice, the leaping of my dog in the grass, the scent of the apricot on the old, red-brick, sun-baked wall, the iridescence of this opal, the sound of the grinding of the pebbles on yonder seashore' (*Essays*, ii, 142). All these things are really different from me, which they would not be if both they and I were merely parts of a self-sufficient, self-subsistent totality with nothing beyond it. Once more, it will be admitted that man does possess at least a dim, confused sense of something ultimate, of some kind of a God, but he derives this not from his own imagination, but 'only on occasion of, together with, in contrast to, well inside this same man's many-levelled, manifold impressions and stimulations—physical, vegetative, psychical, mental, spiritual, as these proceed from realities distinct from himself . . . all operating as parts of a whole to which man is organic' (*Essays*, ii, 143). This dim sense, it is true, does not furnish any clear, stable image of a Perfect Being, but it gives a vague impulsion and unrest, and is met, in real life, by the clear conceptions of the great world-religions.

(c) Pantheism is unsatisfactory in view of the terrible reality of error and evil. These facts, it is true, present the greatest theoretical difficulty which Theism also has to meet, but Pantheism, while seeming to surmount it, only renders it more formidable; for 'if the world as it stands and not an Ultimate Reality behind it is perfect' there is no escape from the conclusion that evil is part of a perfect world, which is equivalent to saying that what we regard as evil is really good. On the other hand, if evil is regarded as something which has to be overcome in real life, Pantheism is powerless. Nothing but Theism, and in particular Christianity, can provide the motive power which alone can transmute it (*Essays*, i, 93).

(d) The tendency of Pantheistic thought is to 'flatten out' the world (*Essays*, i, 294), to reduce things to a dead level; but existence is infinitely rich, infinitely varied, on many different levels. Theism must insist on the wholeness and unity of the universe, for if it is the expression of the mind of God, who is the very standard and perfection of unity, it cannot be anything else; but unity is not the same thing as uniformity. The inorganic world, the various stages of organic life, plant, animal, man, and (he adds) 'whatever other organic finite beings may inhabit the other stars', the various grades of instinct or consciousness, are all interlocked, and explicable only in terms of their relationship to other grades, higher or lower; but what characterizes the whole is not uniformity and likeness, but richness and variety. The universe is not an aggregate of similar elements, but an organic whole which, so far from being uniform, displays the most astonishing and perplexing dissimilarity in its different parts (*Essays*, ii, 142).

CHAPTER IV

THE existence of the religious instinct and of great religious systems cannot be denied. How are they to be accounted for? Are they the result of the internal activities of the mind and the emotions operating in accordance with a process of secular, self-sufficient evolution, or of the reaction of the soul of man to stimulations derived from something outside it? In other words, is Religion an illusion—salutary and beautiful, it may be, but essentially a dream—or has it to do with hard facts?

Von Hügel has no use for illusions. If Religion is nothing more, he would have been content to let it go. His writings are full of assertions of its objective validity.

'Religion begins with a full affirmation of Reality.'

'Religion is adoration.'

'Religion, in proportion to its genuine religiousness, always affirms more and other than laws of the mind or impressions of the soul. It ever affirms Reality, a Reality, *the* Reality distinct from ourselves, the Self-subsistent Spirit, God. It is essentially affirmation of Fact, of what *is*, of what aboriginally, supremely *is*.

It is in this sense ontological, metaphysical: it is this, or it is nothing' (*Essays*, ii, 59).

'Religion, even more than all other convictions that claim correspondence with the Real, begins and proceeds and ends with the Given—with existences, realities which environ and penetrate us, and which we have always anew to capture and to combine, to fathom and to comprehend' (Preface to *Essays*, i, p. 13).

He adds to the last of these passages the remark that he 'has never ceased, now for fifty years, wistfully to find this conviction to be somehow rare amongst his fellow-men, even amongst those who are sincerely religious'.

Nothing is more characteristic of von Hügel than his insistence that in religion the soul must look outwards and not inwards, must accept and appropriate what is Given, not set up any sort of image for itself or lose itself in self-induced emotion. Religious experience in his sense of the words is a response to a stimulation from a Source which is external to the soul which experiences it, just as the experience on which science is based is a response to the stimulation of an objectively existent world. It is of course possible for the mind to misinterpret its experience, and it will need all the help which systems of religious philosophy or the great Institutional Religions can give towards a true interpretation. Here lies a vast field for the activities of the intellect; and this is the intellect's true function in religion—not to build up an imaginary system (which no doubt it has the power to do) based upon the emotional and intellectual prepossessions of the individual, but taking the whole range of spiritual experience as manifested not merely in the individual himself but in other individuals and in history as well, and in particular in the great religious thinkers of the world, to elicit those common features which are independent of individual proclivities and are inexplicable unless they are referred to some common underlying Reality as their source.

This must not be taken to imply that the particular experience of an individual, however novel or unparalleled, may not be true and genuine in the sense that it is a real reaction to an external Reality. The whole possibility of any advance to a higher grade of spiritual knowledge rests upon the supposition that the individual and the race are continually acquiring fresh experience to form the basis of new knowledge which is to correct and enlarge knowledge already attained. What concerned von Hügel was that so-called religious experience, which history has often shown to be fallacious and misleading to a high degree, should be tested by reference to some standard external to the experiencing soul. The mind has the power to weave systems for itself out of experience, real or supposed, and those systems will inevitably be coloured by the subjective likes and dislikes of the individual. Here lies the danger which seemed to him so supreme. If truth is the object of religious knowledge, as of any other kind,

something more is needed in a system than an ideal
consistency which may commend itself to such intellect,
or an appeal which may satisfy such emotions as the
individual happens to possess. We need to be sure that
the webs which we weave are not the mere creations
of imagination, however refined or exalted, but that
they have their counterpart in, and are from beginning
to end elicited by, something in the creation of which
imagination has no part. That they have an existence
of a sort of their own in the mind is undeniable: the
question for von Hügel is whether they are or are not
subject to any check or control from outside. If not,
they are not in touch with Reality as he understood it.

This is the thought which lies at the bottom of von
Hügel's reiterated assertions that all mere systems of
Ethics or Morals fall short of Religion inasmuch as
they never penetrate beyond the region of what *ought
to be* into the region of what *is*. 'Religion,' he writes,
has to do 'not with the production of what ought to
be, but with fear, love, adoration of what already is'
(*Essays*, i, 23). There is room for Ethics inside a self-
centred process of evolution, for Ethics have an obvious
survival value for the race, and inasmuch as the good of
the whole is more important than the particular good
of the separate parts, a system so evolved may furnish
a sort of sanction for unselfishness and even conceivably
give rise to a sense of absolute obligation. But the
question in religion is not whether I do, or do not do,
what I ought in conformity with a fixed standard, but

how far I am in touch with a Supreme Reality for which or for whom 'oughtness' and 'isness', to use his own rather uncouth terms, are the same thing (*Essays*, ii, 248). Here he definitely parts company with Kant, for whom Ethics is the fundamental science, and Religion provides a metaphysical guarantee of the victory of the moral order over the phenomenal world. Kant was right to lay stress upon the indefeasible authority of conscience; but for him conscience meant the determination of the will by the purely practical reason. Whatever necessity it carries is subjective in origin. But for von Hügel there is something behind conscience. The doing of what is right is one of the ways in which man establishes contact with the Supreme Being, because it brings man into conformity with His will. It conducts him towards the Presence, and it is indispensable in that respect, but it does not define his attitude when he is there or indicate the nature of possible communion. That is the office of Religion.

But it may be urged from the Subjectivist side that there are certain features of the religious consciousness itself and facts in the history of religion which militate against the belief in an objective Supreme Reality. If such a Reality—in particular if a Personal God—exists, might it not have been expected that human intimations of His nature would have shown some sort of uniformity? How are we to account for their endless variations? The comparative study of religions

E

shows how many and how deep those variations are: individuals professing the same religion differ widely in their apprehension of what seems vital: the same religion or the same individual presents different aspects at different times. Does not all this look more like an evolution from inside than a reaction to an external influence? Moreover, there are religions of a low type which have features which are repulsive and degrading, and even the great religions of the highest type, such as the religion of the Hebrews, in their earlier stages manifest frequent violations of what are understood later on to be fundamental moral and spiritual duties and qualities. There is also the 'crude childishness' which disfigures so much of popular religion. There is so much that seems unworthy. Again, if religion deals with what is objectively real, how is it that it clashes or seems to clash with certain apparently well-grounded postulates or conclusions of natural science or mental philosophy? Why has it so often turned away from other human interests or activities, or else attempted to dominate them and had to confess that it was in the wrong?

This is a formidable indictment, and von Hügel deals with it in the two important papers on 'Religion and Illusion' and 'Religion and Reality'.

(1) 'Doubtless more or less self-delusion in religion,' he says, 'must at all times have occurred, and must still be occurring, both in individuals and even in the larger groups; and doubtless, had religion never existed, certain

special kinds of self-delusion would not have operated amongst men' (*Essays*, i, 47). But there is nothing unreasonable in this. We find the same bewildering variation, both simultaneous and successive, in Ethics, Politics, Natural Science itself—'similar childish beginnings and similar slow and precarious growth'. We cannot deny the trustworthiness of religious experience unless we become sceptics in those other sciences also. The subject-matter of religion is 'richer' and the apprehension of it therefore more difficult, but the presumption that it is trustworthy is the same. Science, Art, Ethics, Politics, and Religion stand or fall together in this respect.

(2) We have to face the fact that the earlier and cruder forms of religion do incorporate widespread violations of the later and higher ideals, and also that, where improvement occurs, much of it seems often to be attributable to the growth of civilization and of a humane spirit, sometimes in acute conflict with the religious ideas prevailing at the time. But the scantiest acquaintance with what has happened in the past is sufficient to show that religion manifests growth much in the same way as the various branches of knowledge, and the fact that it does so is not a more fatal fault in it than it is in them. Moreover man's whole nature hangs together: the religious side of it cannot be isolated without damage to the personality as a whole. He receives intimations of Objective Reality through 'a whole mass of energies belonging to different levels

and values' (*Essays*, i, 46), and though Religion furnishes the deepest of them, none of the others can be left out of account, just as the Æsthetic sense which conveys direct intimations of the Beautiful rests upon the operation of numerous other energies ranging from the senses up to the highest mental processes. The argument implied in this last statement appears to be that since all the activities of man's composite nature point to the existence of an Ultimate Reality from which they derive a knowledge of that Reality in their own various fashions, their joint contributions to that knowledge form a common stock, and it is not surprising if some are found at times to correct error or supplement inadequacy in others, and to raise the whole to a higher level.

(3) The difficulties attendant upon the supposed conflict between Religion on one side and Philosophy and Science on the other are thus stated by von Hügel with trenchant and uncompromising sincerity (*Essays*, i, 29): 'What is the worth of such superhuman affirmations, if we get into trouble and deadlocks of all sorts as soon as ever we seriously begin to apply them to anything— as soon as ever we deduce, anticipate, or test any scientific method or fact from them? Can affirmations be true, and indeed the deepest of all truths, if they have carefully to be kept out of the reach of all tests of their truth? Is a position bearable which forces us either to limit or vitiate our sciences . . . or to emasculate our religion?'

He takes the chief difficulties to be four in number, connected with the conceptions of Revelation, Miracle, Creation, and Personality. We have already indicated his treatment of the question of Personality. Miracle will be considered in the next chapter in connection with his idea of the Supernatural. Revelation may be reserved until later. Here I will only touch briefly upon the conception of Creation, which has been thought to be incompatible with the modern theory of Evolution. Von Hügel's argument is that in the first place 'no sheer beginnings, however much we may attempt to conceive them in terms and images of the latest Natural Science, are picturable or clearly thinkable by us at all' (*Essays*, i, 48). Yet, on the other hand, all existing things, even the Universe as a whole, bear marks of having had a beginning: we cannot conceive of them without. Natural Science can only start with 'already extant diffused matter', and tends to speak of it as though it were grouped into combinations producing more and more complex results by purely immanental forces; but in itself it can teach us nothing of the eternity or non-eternity of matter. Science must have something to work upon. Where did it come from, and when did it come? We can only picture its origin in terms of space and time, as though it came from somewhere and at some point of time. That is to say, we try to import into our idea of a condition of things which *ex hypothesi* excludes space and time and the very ideas of space and time

themselves. The doctrine of Creation, rightly understood, is an acknowledgment that any attempt to
explain the origin of things in such terms is doomed to
failure. Science has no quarrel with the idea of
Creation, so long as it confines itself to its own range
which is limited by the conceptions of time and space:
nor has the idea of Creation, which lies outside spatial
and temporal limits, any quarrel with what goes on
within those limits. The theory of Evolution, in so
far as it has been proved to be true, lies within the
range of Science. It 'gives us, not the ultimate
why, but the intermediate how' (*Essays*, i, 49). It
throws light upon the method, but it has nothing to
say as to the ultimate origin.

The origin of the Subjectivist temper of mind
against which so much of von Hügel's polemic is
directed may be traced back to that great reaction
against externalism the first stirrings of which made
themselves felt in the fourteenth century and which in
the fifteenth ushered in the modern world. It began
with Literature and Art in the Renaissance: it invaded
Religion at the time of the Reformation: it overflowed
into Politics: it attained unrestricted self-expression at
the time of the French Revolution: it underlay the
whole of the rationalistic movement of the nineteenth
century, and it is still strong and confident. Lord
Acton was accustomed to draw a hard and fast line
between the old and the new.

'The modern age,' he says, 'did not proceed from

the medieval by normal succession, with outward tokens of legitimate descent. Unheralded, it founded a new order of things, under a law of innovation, sapping the ancient reign of continuity. In those days Columbus subverted the notions of the world, and reversed the conditions of production, wealth, and power; in those days Machiavelli released government from the restraint of law; Erasmus diverted the current of ancient learning from profane into Christian channels; Luther broke the chain of authority and tradition at the strongest link; and Copernicus erected an invincible power that set for ever the mark of progress upon the time that was to come' (*Inaugural Lecture on the Study of Modern History*, p. 3).

Von Hügel was content with a less cataclysmic interpretation of history. He went farther back for the first signs of the new spirit, and would not have acknowledged so abrupt a chasm between the old and the new. The oscillations of a pendulum, even when violent and irregular, are the expression of a continuous motion, and it is the business of the philosopher to demonstrate the continuity. But there is a broad difference between the outlook of the modern and that of the medieval world, and the difference began with the emergence of an independent spirit in vigorous hostility against the tyranny of the external, against the sacrifice of the spirit to the letter, of the substance to the form. In philosophy Aristotle and Aquinas were superseded by Bacon, and in religion Christianity tended more and more to become identified with mere Soteriology.

There are signs that the strength of this great movement of thought is beginning to fade. Newman long ago entered a vehement protest against what he called Liberal Protestantism, and von Hügel was not alone in his antipathy to exaggerated Subjectivism. On the Continent to-day there is a strong reaction in some quarters in favour of the Realism which he proclaimed as the necessary foundation of religion. The dominance of the subjective outlook shows signs of drawing to its close.

The special interest of his own position is that he combines a whole-hearted dislike of the one-sidedness of some manifestations of the modern spirit with a no less whole-hearted acceptance of the principle of the application of modern methods to the study of religion.

CHAPTER V

THE two most important distinctions with which any religion of a highly developed type has to deal are the distinction between the Natural and the Supernatural and that between Good and Evil. The latter at first sight seems to be the more fundamental. It is hard to imagine any deeper difference than that between Good and Bad, even if you admit that there is not always a consensus of opinion as to what is good and what is bad. But we find von Hügel repeatedly asserting that the former is the more important. In what sense is this true? Good and Evil are clearly contradictory. What did he conceive to be the relation between the Natural and the Supernatural?

We will begin with his own statements of the relation between the two problems.

'Man is incurably *amphibious*; he belongs to Two Worlds—to two sets of duties, needs, and satisfactions —to the Visible or This World, and to the Invisible or the Other World. This duality precedes and reaches farther than even the duality of Good and Evil' (*Essays*, ii, 247).

'What concerns us here is not the Supernatural in

63

its contrast and conflict with sin and sinful human nature; but the Supernatural as distinct from healthy Nature, and the inter-aid and yet tension at work between them.   It certainly looks as though the dread battle between the simply Bad and the Good of whatsoever kind were the more promising mental problem for us, just as this battle is the more pressing practical concern of us all.   Yet I have come to the conclusion . . . that, not the contrast between sin and virtue, but the difference between Nature and Supernature can furnish a solid starting-point for the recovery, the resuscitation of religion, as by far the richest, the most romantic, the most entrancing and emancipating fact and life extant or possible anywhere for man' (*Essays*, i, 279).

'The widest and most primitive contrasts here are, not Sin and Redemption (though these of course remain), but Nature (however good in its kind) and Supernature' (*Essays*, i, 88).

And he speaks of 'the noble fullness of insight offered to us all by St. Thomas's assignation of the first place to the distinction between Nature and Supernature, in lieu of that between Fallen Nature and Redemption' (*Essays*, i, 164).

Now we may notice to begin with:

(1) That the sense in which he uses the words is not that in which they are most commonly used.   In ordinary language 'Natural', when contrasted with

'Supernatural', most frequently seems to imply the presence of evil in some degree: it is often used in Theology as if it were practically synonymous with evil. But von Hügel is speaking of a nature which is 'healthy', which is good. The distinction is not between bad and good, but between two things which are both good.

(2) That this is not a modern doctrine, but derives from Aquinas and the Golden Age of Medievalism. It is, as he says elsewhere (*Essays*, i, 214), 'the fundamental axiom of all the teaching' of that great thinker, and was 'all-pervasive' in those great days.

According to this conception there is nothing intrinsically evil in the Natural. Nature is good: the material world is good: Art, Science, and Literature are good: man's activities in society and in the State are good: ordinary, everyday life is good. There is a Natural Ethic, which is good so far as it goes. There is even a Natural Religion, also good so far as it goes, though only leading up to a vague, undefined Theism. Man might have been left at this level and all would still have been good, for the evil which appears in the Natural Order is an intrusive element, not part of the fundamental constitution of things. If such a purely natural outlook, quite unmixed with the supernatural, existed anywhere, the prospect after death would be simply the continuation for ever of this natural goodness, 'with the dim background of God, less suffering, offences against this rational code, and death'. It is the 'sane and sensible, but dry and shallow outlook' of 'Bentham amongst recent Englishmen and Confucius amongst the great ancient and non-European moral and religious leaders' (*Essays*, i, 282).

But man has not been so left. There is a higher level to which he may rise, and if and as he becomes conscious of it the obligation to ascend is laid upon him. Thus there are two grades or stages in the apprehension of the Supreme Reality. The higher, which is better, presupposes the lower, which is good, and the two are dovetailed and interlocked together. There may be sporadic supernatural experiences or actions in a life which is normally on the natural level; and on the other hand the supernatural rests upon and is evoked by endless interactions and tensions with the natural. Both orders 'spring from the same God, at two levels of His action' (*Essays*, i, 96).

The Supernatural in this sense is to be distinguished from the Miraculous. 'By supernatural,' he writes, 'we here mean nothing preternatural, nothing even essentially miraculous, nothing that men, who are at all complete according to man's supernatural call and awakeness, cannot, or do not, experience' (*Essays*, i, 197). He refers to the controversy between Bossuet and Fénelon as to the nature of the spiritual life, and ranges himself definitely on the side of Fénelon who declared that the whole of that life 'from its rudimentary beginnings up to its very highest grades and developments is essentially and increasingly supernatural, but at no point essentially miraculous' (*Essays*, i, 279). From this it follows that the course of the spiritual life can be to some extent foretold, and certain great laws and characteristics of its operation in the past discovered, though a limit is set by the extremely complicated nature of the subject-matter and the need of the utmost sincerity and sensitiveness in the observer.

But this is not the case with the Miraculous; and in the essay on 'Religion and Reality' we have an indication of what he meant by this ambiguous term, when dissociated from elementary and unworthy conceptions and made available for the higher religions and the purer types of religious experience (*Essays*, i, 57). He regards it as characterized by 'three vivid, independent apprehensions'. (1) The consciousness that something *unique* is being experienced or produced in the particular apprehending soul. (2) The consciousness 'that this unique experience comes from the One Divine Spirit to this particular human spirit'. (3) The apprehension that this effect of Spirit upon spirit is not restricted to the human spirit alone, but may and does affect the phenomenal world—'the body and its psychical, indeed even its physical conditions and environment, and the visible exterior conditions and history of mankind'. He proceeds to argue, if I have rightly interpreted a somewhat obscure passage, that as you ascend from a lower to a higher grade in the scale of Reality the sense of uniqueness increases: there is a 'nearer and nearer approach to the Concrete

Universal, to the unique embodiment of an universally valuable type'. The term miraculous is apparently to be applied to an occasion or an experience in which that approach is felt to be so close that the uniqueness of the embodiment of the Concrete Universal is vividly realized. This is a metaphysical analysis of what he believed to be a common and permanent experience of mankind.

At the same time he is careful to guard against the difficulties suggested by the misconception of what a miracle means. Those difficulties only arise when the three central apprehensions are interpreted as implying that 'the spiritual or psychical or physical effects of Miracle constitute direct breaches within (as it were) the phenomenal rind and level of natural reality—breaches which can be strictly demonstrated to be such by Natural Science itself' (*Essays*, i, 58). Thus he repudiates the old idea that a Miracle is a violation of the order of Nature, which has served so many centuries as a proof of the existence of an Author of Nature. Science, he argues, can never demonstrate that an occurrence *is* a breach of natural laws, for it is restricted to its own level and sphere in which strict continuity and repetititive law reign supreme. Where there is no law, there is no science: within the scientific sphere there can be no violations of order. Whatever it is, a miracle cannot be that.

It appears then that von Hügel conceived a miracle as an occurrence, inward or outward, which is, and is consciously apprehended as, unique in the most complete sense of the word; but that, so far from constituting a breach or violation of any lower kind of order, it is in essence a sort of intensive realization of the supreme principle of order beneath which all other lower kinds must be subsumed and which gives to them such degree of permanence and reality as they possess.   In contrast with this he seems to have thought of the Supernatural as a steady, all-pervasive influence, always at work, always in multitudinous ways penetrating, or seeking to penetrate, the Natural and to raise it to a higher level.   Its manifestations vary in vividness and intensity, but there is nothing essentially catastrophic about them.   In spite of the strong mystical element in his character he distrusted dramatic spiritual experiences —mainly, I think, because they seem to involve an exaggerated subjectivism.   Thus we find him, in the course of some remarks delivered at a meeting of the Committee to inquire into Religion in the Army in 1917—informal it is true, but not the less sincere on that account—saying: 'Let us not underline St. Paul too much; he is the first of our cataclysmic converts. Do take him, for Heaven's sake, *cum grano*' (*Letters*, p. 65).

We are led on to inquire what are the characteristics of the Supernatural as manifested in human life and action?   It must be remembered that we are still thinking of the Natural as essentially good and capable of becoming better, and are not yet concerned with the

complication introduced by the presence of evil.   He
has sketched in outline the effect of the Supernatural
upon the great natural virtues (*Essays*, i, 285 ff.).   It
raises them to a heroic standard.   This statement
must not be misunderstood.   The quality of the supernatural is always heroic, but the material in which it
is manifested is itself not always or ordinarily heroic
but often humble and even trivial.   If 'it means high
heroism it also means hospitable homeliness: it means
the Alpine Uplands—the edelweiss and the alpen rose
—as well as the Lombard Plains with their corn and
their potatoes; it means poetry and prose, a mighty
harmony and a little melody; or rather it means, taken
as a complete whole, an organ recital, with the *grand
jeu* stop of Supernature drawn out full and all the pipes
of Nature responding in tones each necessary in its
proper place, yet each sweeter and richer than its own
simply natural self' (*Essays*, i, 284).   There is, it is
true, a natural heroism of acts which conform to a
recognized external standard; but the heroism of the
Supernatural, though often manifested in acts acknowledged by the opinion of the world to be heroic, consists
in an interior attitude of the soul in face of all occasions,
great or small.   It finds expression in sublime instances
of self-sacrifice, but it is also present in and adds a lustre
to the 'mild concerns of ordinary life'.

In human experience, as things stand, the passage
from the Natural to the Supernatural, the attainment
of the heroic temper, is a costly process, involving pain,

effort, and distress. No one has insisted more strongly than von Hügel that the man who aspires to the attainment of the higher level with the comforting expectation that he has a smooth and even path before him is likely to be woefully mistaken. And the question has often been asked—most often, perhaps, by those whose aspiration is most sincere—whether it is possible to imagine a state of things in which goodness, and in particular the higher grades of goodness, is realizable without the presence and the conquest of evil. We think of a heroic act, even of an ordinary good act, as in some sense a victory. What becomes of it if there is nothing to overcome? This is a question which needs an answer, for in default of one there appears to be no escape from an ultimate dualism. We will consider it more in detail later on, but we may say here that the thesis that there is a natural order which is good and a supernatural order which is better, and also the possibility of passing from one to another, amounts to an assertion that such a state of things is not only imaginable but actually existent. If there were anything *essentially* evil in the natural order good could only be realized at the cost of a conflict and a victory: if the evil which is admittedly present is not essentially inherent, but intrusive, it is possible to imagine a universe purged of evil in which good would have free play, but the good would not be less good on that account.

This conception of the relation between the Natural

F

and the Supernatural carries with it the Catholic doctrine of the two levels in the moral life, which is a suggested solution of what von Hügel calls 'the most difficult of all the problems raised by the Christian Ethic—that as to the precise character of its opposition to the world' (*Essays*, i, 160).   The problem is that, if the exalted ideal of conduct implied in Christianity is set forth as the goal of the whole world's achievement, the great majority of mankind, including many who certainly seem to live ordinarily good lives, never have attained it and, as far as can be seen, never are likely to.   What is to be thought of them?   Is Christianity only the religion of the elect?   Is there no alternative between a world of saints, which is unimaginable, and a world composed of a sort of spiritual aristocracy of saints and a multitude of sinners?   A complete solution of this difficulty is beyond our grasp: but if there is, as well as a higher level which is best, a lower level which is also good, we get what seems to be a more adequate explanation of the facts than any theory of an absolute division into two classes can offer.   The two levels, on this theory, are interlocked: the higher is super-imposed upon the lower, which it presupposes and which it transforms, sometimes by a continuous action, some-times by sporadic manifestations.   And it is to be noted that this transformation may occur in the case of an individual without his full consciousness of it.   'A man,' he says, 'may perform a truly supernatural act, or be in a genuinely supernatural condition of soul, and yet may possess, at the time or even generally, only the most dim and confused—a quite inadequate— theology' (*Essays*, i, 280). Or to take a more extreme case, he says of 'a Positivist of European renown,' whose life had been occupied until shortly before its close in an intensive propaganda of unbelief but had all along been maintained at an exceptionally high ethical level, that 'apparently a man can be in good faith, at least for many years, in the denial of even the very rudiments of Theism' (*Essays*, i, 4). The two passages quoted only suggest, directly, that a consciousness of the Supernatural is not an invariable condition of its presence; but they seem to imply the belief that the passage out of the Natural is not necessarily cataclysmic, as it would be if the two orders were antipathetic, and that there is a goodness on the natural level which is related to the Christian ideal as the incomplete is related to the complete. We find the same idea underlying his conception of the relation between Christianity and other religions.

The reiterated insistence upon the importance of a revival of this medieval doctrine at the present time is a natural outcome of von Hügel's optimism—an optimism founded upon a combination of prophetic fervour and robust common sense. The pall of gloom which has settled upon so much of popular religion since the Reformation needs to be lifted: the sense of monotony, dullness, and oppression needs to be dissipated: the depressing effect which the discussion of religious questions or the very mention of religion has upon the man in the street needs to be counteracted. As long as the mind is preoccupied with the idea of the prevalence of evil and regards religion primarily as a means of escape, this attitude is more or less inevitable. But religion is more than mere Soteriology. It is, or ought to be, 'by far the richest, the most romantic, the most entrancing and emancipating fact and life extant or possible anywhere for man' (*Essays*, i, 280). Religion, in spite of self-sacrifice, is a happy affair. 'The Divinely-intended End of our Life is Joy overflowing and infinite,' though it is 'closely connected with a noble asceticism' (*Essays*, ii, 239). The doctrine that there is a Natural Order which is good as well as the Supernatural seemed to him to provide a much needed antidote to the sour, suspicious temper which looks askance at everything not definitely and consciously recognized as religious, and to the pessimistic timidity which refuses an open-hearted welcome to the gifts of nature, and the natural virtues and the achievements of progress and civilization, through an uneasy apprehension that they are in some more or less undefined way necessarily tainted and corrupt.

This pronounced dislike to a hard and fast line between the Natural and the Supernatural, the Secular and the Religious, is noticeable in the series of letters to his niece. These include suggestions for an elaborate and comprehensive course of study—a sort of ideal education in religious thought; but he is definitely afraid of any conscious preoccupation with the religious side alone. Secular literature is to be read, not as something which religion may possibly tolerate, or over which it may throw the ægis of a condescending patronage, but as the natural expression of, and as necessary for the comprehension of, those among man's varied thoughts, aspirations, and activities which are not specifically religious but which no religion that is not emasculated can ignore. Man is body as well as soul. Psychology and Epistemology prove that sense stimulations and impressions are the necessary conditions of mental presentations and convictions (*Essays*, ii, 106). Facts in the phenomenal world, historical persons, and happenings, all that man does and thinks and wants are the material on which religion works and which serve to support it by multitudinous tensions and interactions. Human nature is a whole.

But there is another side to all this. If it is good that the young man should rejoice in his youth, John Gilpin in the activities of an ordinary citizen, the man of action in what he does, the man of words in what he says or writes, the thinker in his thought, without any *arrière-pensée*, that is not a sufficient account of the whole of life. The satisfaction of man's natural impulses and instincts on a normal level is not enough to content him, and the more refined and sensitive his nature, the greater is his discontent. There is what is called in modern language an 'urge' upwards, which creates a sort of dislocation, so that the lower level, even when considered as unaffected by evil, is often found to be in conflict, sometimes in violent conflict, with the higher.   Hence the contrast between the 'this world' or 'domestic' type and the 'other world' or 'heroic' type of action and character.   Acquiescence in a low standard when a higher standard is within reach is the betrayal of a great trust.   In spite of the doctrine that both levels are good, von Hügel often speaks as if life or thought upon the lower level were intolerable.   So, no doubt, it is, or ought to be, for any one who is aware of the contrast between them. Moreover, in actual life the question is complicated by the presence of evil.   Even if it found no place in the original order, it is there now, and the choice presented to man, as matters stand, is often the choice, not between something which is good and something which is better, but between something which is good and something which is the opposite.

CHAPTER VI

THE PROBLEM OF EVIL

If there is so much that is good and beautiful and true in nature and in human nature, which may, which must, be accepted and welcomed and used unless religion is to be reduced to the spiritless, submissive pessimism of the Buddhist or the nobler but defiant pessimism of the Stoic, what is the nature of the evil which obtrudes itself everywhere, which refuses to be explained away, the range of which only seems to grow wider the further the analysis of the phenomena of the physical, mental, and spiritual life is carried? Obviously there is a sense in which all is *not* right with the world.

Here is the greatest theoretic difficulty against all Theism—'the reality of evil with its brutal facts and baffling obscurities' (*Essays*, i, 119). 'We fail,' von Hügel says, 'in our attempts at explaining how or why, with an All-knowing, All-powerful, and All-loving God there can be evil at all' (*Mystical Element*, ii, 292). He has no solution of the problem to offer, but he has treated two aspects of the subject in some detail in the section on 'Mysticism and the Question of Evil' in the

Mystical Element (ii, 290 ff.), in the letter to a bereaved parent printed in the first series of *Essays* (pp. 98–116), and in the address on 'Suffering and God' in the second series (pp. 167–213). Even if evil, suffering, and sin are taken as difficulties which are possibly incapable of any complete solution, they do not of themselves, he argues, abolish the evidential value discovered to attach to the superhuman intimations of religion (*Essays*, i, 43).

He will have nothing to do with any attempt to explain them away. 'Evil and the evil effects of Evil are not the mere absence of Good and of the effects of Good; Evil is in truth a force and positive—it is an actual perversion and not an abolition of the efficacious will' (*Essays*, i, 214). It is a 'dread reality'. He attacks Mysticism in its exaggerated form as tending to deny all positive character to Evil. This tendency is seen at its strongest in Plotinus, whom he calls 'the prince of mystical philosophers' (*Mystical Element*, ii, 293). It is marked in the mystical side of Augustine, in spite of his acute preoccupation in other moods with the doctrine of Original Sin: it is found in Aquinas and Eckhart: it disfigures the philosophies of Hegel and Schleiermacher: it is pushed to its logical conclusion by Spinoza. On the other side he quotes with approval a statement of Kant that human nature is so corrupt that a thinking man might be tempted 'to turn away his look from it altogether, lest he fall himself into another vice, that of hatred of mankind' (*Mystical Element*, ii, 296), and another statement of

Eucken, that 'the mysterious fact of Evil, as a positive opposition to good, has never ceased to occupy the highest minds. The concept of moral guilt cannot be got rid of, try as we may'. That is to say, there is something which has to be taken into account which is beyond mere selfishness, mere self-indulgence, mere weakness—something of a malevolent type, an evil disposition which manifests itself in hatred and envy even where self-interest is not touched and in a sort of satisfaction found in destroying or disfiguring what is good. Evil is active, positive, malicious, rebellious.

Hence we find him insisting that Christianity sees deeper into the nature of moral evil than the Stoic or other philosophical systems because it regards Pride, Vanity, Self-sufficiency—what he calls 'the solipsism of the spirit' (*Mystical Element*, ii, 301), as the typical sins, rather than the sensual tendencies proceeding from the body. This is not the popular estimate of the relative importance of these failings, which tends to glorify respectability and pass lightly over what are in reality more heinous forms of guilt, but the popular estimate he regarded as wrong. There is a sort of natural level of human action, and there are 'aberrations' both below and above this level (*Essays*, i, 11). Aberrations on the lower side, the side of the body, are easily recognized and generally condemned: aberrations on the upper side are obscured by a blindness which he thinks is largely due to the predominant preoccupation with the triumphant progress of knowledge and science, but they are more serious because they have their origin not in the weakness which fails to withstand temptation, but in a positive perversity of the will. So far as aberrations of the first kind are concerned he acknowledges that the attempts which have been made to explain moral evil as atavism on evolutionary lines are 'of great psychological interest and of much pedagogic help' (*Essays*, i, 10), but the explanation of pride and self-centredness as depending in the last resort as truly upon the animal descent as do impurity, gluttony, and sloth, 'simply will not work'. Here it is a case, not of falling back, but of defiance and revolt. The evil will is in active opposition.

What then is the position of evil in the world? Whence did it come, and when? If the relation of the natural to the supernatural is what von Hügel believed it to be, it is not inherent in the natural. However obvious it may be that the progressive realization of what is good involves under present conditions a war to the knife between the flesh and the spirit, the flesh is not nature: it is corrupt nature. The war is a war for the expulsion of an invader: evil is something which has intruded into a universe which was originally and remains essentially good. Speculation as to its origin is natural and inevitable but only serves to emphasize the difficulty of the inquiry, and modern evolutionary ideas have not made things any easier. The orthodox doctrine of an original state of innocence and a single historical lapse which has left the world vitiated and corrupt seemed to von Hügel to need modification in the light of modern science. He goes so far as to say: 'The ever-accumulating number and weight of even the most certain facts and most moderate inductions of Anthropology and Ethnology are abolishing all evidential grounds for holding a primitive high level of human knowledge and innocence, and a single sudden plunge into a fallen estate, apparently against all our physiological, psychological, historical evidences and analogies (which all point to a gradual rise from lowly beginnings), and are reducing such a conception to a pure postulate of Theology' (*Mystical Element*, ii, 299).

But he notes that these sciences leave undisturbed the orthodox belief that if mankind as a whole, or the human individual, are to rise in the spiritual scale, they can only do it at the price of the elimination of what is lower with the help of what is higher. Evil is from this point of view a sort of anachronism, the resistance to the Divine force that makes for righteousness, and the story of the Fall is a representation of the undoubted fact of this continuous resistance in the form of a historical event. But sin is not a mere anachronism: it is not a throwing-back on the lines of what occurs in the evolution of the organic world of nature. It is not an accident in a progress towards a more perfect order to be realized in the future, but a deliberate interference with that progress, and such interference can only come from something which is external to and antagonistic to the order which is in process of realization, that is from an evil will.

We have already seen how profoundly antagonistic von Hügel is to the popular idea of the Free Will, the notion that it is a sort of indeterminate, independent entity which has the power of choosing arbitrarily between different courses of action which may be good or bad as the case may be. He substitutes for that the distinction between Perfect and Imperfect Freedom. 'The possibility of evil arises,' he says, 'not from Freedom as such, but from the imperfection of the human kind of freedom—the Liberty of Choice' (*Essays*, i, II). 'Perfect Liberty consists in willing fully and spontaneously the behests of a perfect nature and in the incapacity to will otherwise. Hence the more arbitrary the act, the less really free it is' (*Essays*, i, 17). This doctrine must be true 'unless God, who cannot sin, is a slave, and human souls become less free in proportion as they grow less liable to moral evil'. Theories of religion which teach 'an arbitrary will in God, answered by acts of sheer will in man' intrinsically contradict the rationalities of life and of the world, as in the case of Luther, Descartes, and Pascal. Even Kant, whose doctrine of the Categorical Imperative is a noble expression of the fact that on any one occasion there is only one thing which is definitely right, erred when he denied the connection so clearly proclaimed by Plato and Aristotle between Virtue and the Highest Good, between Morality and Happiness. Morality is not a matter of the imposition of an arbitrary, external standard of action or feeling. When what is good is actualized in man, or indeed anywhere in the universe of created things, that means that the end or aim of his existence is being realized. His whole nature hangs together, and good is organic to that whole, not something superimposed or introduced from outside. The trouble is not that man is essentially bad and needs to be inoculated with good, but that through the weakness or perversity of his will he cannot rise to, or deliberately rejects, the good which he was intended to realize and the position which he was intended to fill.

It is clear that a man's whole outlook on life will be deeply affected according as he takes the position that human nature is essentially good and evil an intrusion, or the position that it is essentially bad and good an intrusion. The scale will come down either on the side of Optimism or of Pessimism. Von Hügel, intensely hostile to the shallow sort of optimism which cries out 'Peace' because it cannot or will not see that there is a war, rested in quiet and robust confidence upon that deeper kind which is inspired by the conviction that, whatever appearances suggest, the ultimate issue must be good.

There is a third position which it is possible to adopt in this matter of Evil, that human nature was originally essentially good, but that it has now become essentially bad. This has profoundly influenced Christian thought, especially since the Reformation, in the form of the doctrines of a single historical lapse from a primitive innocence and of Original Sin. The former, we have seen, von Hügel believed to be in process of reduction by modern science to 'a pure postulate of Theology'. The latter, he acknowledges, 'remains a grave difficulty', but he calls attention to the fact that 'the acute form given to the doctrine by Augustine has never been finally accepted by the Catholic Roman Church' (*Mystical Element*, ii, 300), and he quotes a statement of Dr. F. R. Tennant that 'in this respect the Roman theology is more philosophical than that of the symbols of Protestant Christendom'.

When we come to the question of Pain and Suffering, we find von Hügel completely out of sympathy with the attempts which have been made to explain them as the necessary condition of the attainment of good which without them would not have been realized. 'Suffering,' he says, 'is intrinsically an evil' (*Essays*, ii, 199). There are two points of view which need to be kept distinct. On the one hand the pain and misery in the world seem incompatible with the belief in an All-merciful and All-powerful God, and man either revolts against them or acquiesces in sullen, stoic endurance. At all events suffering seems an unmitigated evil. On the other hand it is undeniable that suffering of mind or body is often the occasion of the attainment of a higher ethical and spiritual level, and that the highest levels have been sometimes attained when the suffering was deepest and keenest. In these cases the evil seems to be a good in disguise. Von Hügel's answer to this is that the rebellion is natural, that suffering merely *as such* cannot soften or widen, but only 'harden, narrow, and embitter' (*Essays*, i, 110). If its effects are good, that is not because there is anything good in suffering, but because there is a Power which is able to transmute it.

No one questions the fact that the passage through suffering may, and often does, purify and elevate the character, in other words that it often is a condition of the realization of a higher good. But suffering is very common, if not universal, and its good effects are very common too. Is it not possible that it may be, not merely a condition, but a *necessary* condition? This is a theory which appears to commend itself to some modern apologists of Christianity. Thus Canon Streeter has written (*Reality*, p. 223):

'A world in which there was no conflict and no risk would be a world in which the heroic quality in man could never be called forth. A world from which suffering or failure were completely absent would be one in which compassion and mutual aid were absent too. A world in which the innocent never suffered for the follies or the crimes of others, where every one got exactly what he himself deserved, would be a world in which it mattered to no one but a man's own self what he himself or any other did: it would be a world where responsibility, *esprit de corps*, brotherhood were unknown.'

Dr. Temple is still more explicit: 'All attempts to conceive a world in which evil plays no part result in a world profoundly unsatisfying to our highest instincts' (*Christus Veritas*, p. 271).

On these premises there seems to be no escape from the dilemma that we must either give up the idea of a perfectly good world altogether and be prepared to accept that of an eternal war between good and evil, or else maintain that evil is not after all in its essence what we commonly mean by evil, inasmuch as good, or at all events some kinds or degrees of good, cannot be realized without it. But no race of men who ever attained to the idea of a life after death has ever been content without the concept of an Elysium of some sort from which suffering is excluded, nor has any one but a philosopher ever doubted that suffering is an evil, or any one but a Christian Scientist that it is a real evil. *Sub specie aeternitatis* there must be something which is final: one side or the other must be victorious; and if the good is to win, we can only conceive of the final state as one

> Where love is an unerring light
> And joy its own security.

Pain, doubt, degradation, death must have vanished into some lake of fire.

This is the thought which underlies the profound essay on 'Suffering and God' in the second volume of the *Essays and Addresses*, which the editor declares to be the one to which von Hügel himself would have attached the greatest importance.

But if the evil is there, and if it is real evil, how is it to be reconciled with the idea of a God who is both all-good and all-powerful? And how can good ever transmute or annul actualized evil? If it cannot, must there not always be a residuum of evil, and has not God failed of the best? Can what has been be as though it had not been? The philosophy of religion has no answer to give to this. The Theist must rest content with the assurance that, unless his belief in an All-good and All-powerful God is unfounded, the triumph of good will involve the demonstration that all through the Time process the evil was under His control.

In the letter already referred to on the 'Preliminaries of Religious Belief and on the Facts of Suffering, Faith, and Love', von Hügel indicates the temper in which alone this and other such difficulties can be profitably approached.

'I assume you,' he says, 'to be non-contentious and non-controversial; to be athirst for wisdom, not for cleverness; to be humble and simple, or at least to feel a wholesome shame at not being so; to be just *straight*, and anxious for some light, and ready to pay for it and practise it.' . . . 'Drop brain, open wide the soul, nourish the heart, purify and strengthen the will: with this you are sure to grow; without this you are certain to shrink' (*Essays*, i, 98).

G

CHAPTER VII

MODERNISM, in the broad sense in which the word is here used, is no new thing in the history of the world. Origen, in the third century, was a Modernist, so was Erasmus, in the sixteenth. It represents a tendency always at work, but more conspicuous at some times than at others.

Dr. Whitehead, in his little book on *Religion in the Making*, has indicated the reason why such an outlook is inevitable.

'The importance of rational religion in the history of modern culture,' he says, 'is that it stands or falls with its fundamental position; that we know more than can be formulated in one finite systematized scheme of abstractions, however important that scheme may be in the elucidation of some aspect of the order of things' (p. 142).

That is to say, experience is always wider and deeper than any intellectual expression of it can be; but since mankind is always reaching out towards an expression that shall be less inadequate, and since the experience itself is always growing, there is a never-ceasing tension between the standard of formulation already attained

and an ideal standard in the background which is per-
petually urging and thrusting it on. This manifests
itself in religion in the form of strained relations
between dogma and new forms of thought.

'Dogmatic expression,' as Dr. Whitehead says, 'is
necessary. For whatever has objective validity is capable
of partial expression in terms of abstract concepts,
so that a coherent doctrine arises which elucidates
the world beyond the locus of the origin of the dogmas
in question. Also exact statements are the media by
which identical intuitions into the world can be identified amid a wide variety of circumstances' (p. 144).

But 'though dogmas have their measure of truth,
which is unalterable, in their precise forms they are
narrow, limitative, and alterable' (p. 145).

In other words, though the truth expressed remains
true, modifications of the expression may be needed
either to express it better or to include new truth.
Thus there arises a practical problem. Religion cannot
do without these 'intermediate representations of
spiritual truths'. 'They are enshrined,' as Whitehead says, 'in modes of worship, in popular religious
literature, and in art.' How is it possible to handle
popular forms of thought in such a way as to maintain
their vital connection with the fundamental truths
which give all its value to any particular formulation
and at the same time to keep them in touch with the
expansion of knowledge and increasing clarity of
interpretation? The position of the Modernist, using

the word in a broad and non-technical sense, is that there is such a problem and that it has got to be faced.

Here is a description of a little-known Modernist of the fifteenth century which may serve as a broad indication of the temper in which von Hügel thought that this problem should be approached. There was a certain Nicolas, the son of a poor fisherman, born at Kues on the Moselle, who became Dean of Coblenz, of whom he speaks thus:

'Christianity, Neo-Platonism, the Teutonic spirit, the early Renaissance; authority and liberty, society and the individual; the depths of faith, the clarities of reason, the vigour of action, the warm, life-welcoming and life-giving expansion and embrace of love: all these individually great and difficult things met, in a rarely full and perfect degree and manner, in this noble precursor and adumbrator of the modern spirit at its very best and deepest' (*Essays*, ii, 92).

Here we have, not a twentieth-century Modernist —with much of what is called Modernism to-day von Hügel had no sympathy whatever—but a man who faced questions which were 'modern' in his day in the spirit in which questions which are 'modern' now ought to be faced. The essence of that spirit is the open-minded acceptance, the generous welcome, accorded to every expansion of the domain of knowledge, to every enlargement in the sphere of spiritual experience.

The acquisition of new knowledge is always going on, the spiritual outlook is always changing, formulas are always pressing for revision; but the process is not uniform. There are periods when knowledge accumulates not by small increments but in rapidly moving, overwhelming masses, and when a whole new outlook on life clamours insistently for recognition and explanation. At such times the tension between the old and the new becomes acute. We are living in such a period now, and the strain is great. It is no easy matter to readjust without destroying, to substitute for what is known to have served mankind well in the past something which it is hoped may serve mankind better in the present, especially when it affects the deepest and most far-reaching of all human needs. Only those who, in von Hügel's words, 'can bear such high air and such giddy downlooks and outlooks' (*Essays*, ii, 4), can hope to reach a rational comprehension of the phase through which the world is passing. But the phase is a real part of experience: the new knowledge, the changed outlook, are real facts which challenge the attention of philosophy and religion.

Such well-defined periods of unsettlement and transition inevitably elicit and inflame the two contrasted elements which are always present in any body of men or in any individual, the instinct of safety which clings loyally to truth already apprehended, and the instinct of adventure which reaches out to the apprehension of new truth. Established religions seem to enthusiastic followers of the new illumination to be irrevocably committed to 'much that clamours for a large discrimination and restatement', to use von Hügel's words, so that they can no longer give an explicit and definite subscription to the old formulas. Moreover the majority of officials almost inevitably find it difficult to accept, and often exhibit hostility towards, modifications and interpretations of the subject-matter with which they are accustomed to deal, even when it can be proved that such modifications are not in conflict with the fundamental truths which the system in question enshrines. They are accustomed to be on the defence, and the sentinel sometimes discharges his rifle without waiting to see whether the new-comer is in reality a friend or a foe. On the other hand the enthusiasm generated by the presumed escape from a real or supposed oppression, and the sense of emergence into a lighter atmosphere and a freer air, renders the newly emancipated reckless in their dealings with the great systems which have their root in the past. A prisoner who has escaped from a structure which he regards as a Bastille sees nothing for it but to lay the whole level with the ground.

In this clash of tendencies it is not surprising if some of the combatants lose their heads and lose their direction, and make use of language which often tends merely to obscure the issues at stake. Here and there an individual with deeper insight and broader sympathies than the rest towers above the turmoil, and indicates, if he does not fully establish, the lines on which reconciliation and reconstruction is possible.

The unrest of the present day takes two forms. First, the application of the historico-critical method to the study of Christianity has shown that the received opinions upon many points of detail need to be revised. Where is this process to end? There is an uneasy apprehension in many minds, and a cynical assurance in many others, that a solvent has been introduced which will end in the disintegration of the whole structure. Von Hügel quotes (*Letters*, p. 355) a sentence from an article by Miss Maude Petre in the *Hibbert Journal* (April 1922) which gives expression to this fear.

'We have to take count not only of what has been ascertained, but of what at any future date may be ascertained. So that for the believer it is quite useless to establish a satisfactory refuge from criticism so far as it has reached, when he knows that it may, even if it do not eventually, reach much farther still.'

We are not concerned here with any attempt to estimate how far any of the conclusions which have been drawn from the intensive study of the Christian records in the modern scientific spirit are justified by the evidence. But we may note in passing that his answer to Miss Petre is that there is no reason to suppose that the history of the science of Biblical criticism will prove to be different from that of other sciences, natural or historical. As time goes on, errors are eliminated and the science becomes indefinitely enriched, but there is no general collapse. 'The most striking part of the whole affair,' he says, 'is that the general orientation, the large outlines, the predominant facts, remain what and where they were.' He has a strong faith that the operations of the mind and the intuitions of the spirit may be trusted to build up a system which in its essence represents truth, even though it may require to be purged of errors which are the inevitable result of the conditions under which the process of formulation has to be carried out.

But the spirit of the times manifests itself in another form. Many persons who are content to leave the decision as to the credibility of this or that detail of traditional orthodoxy to the experts find themselves entirely alienated from the whole idea of Institutional Religion as they understand it, and as they see it at work around them. Here is a difficulty which goes right down to the roots of the religious life. Von Hügel has himself stated it with the utmost candour and trenchancy in his address on 'Official Authority and Living Religion', written in 1904:

'Does the average educated man, in proportion as he truly and deeply (though perhaps quite partially and intermittently) lives the life of the mind and of the spirit—does he apprehend and discover, feel, think, will, and act; does he suffer, love, rejoice, produce in the same manner, with the same forms and categories, as officialism seems to do and to direct him to do?

The question readily answers itself: there is no kind of similarity here between these two series of activities in any single respect' (*Essays*, ii, 5).

He goes on ruthlessly to draw out the divergence in detail. The man, when he feels deeply, is conscious of something new and original, a sort of Present which transcends time; but Authority can only represent the Previous, the What-has-already-been. The man at such moments is lonely and isolated, estranged from the average of other men and from his own average thoughts and moments; but Authority necessarily deals with the Average. It is Philistine: it represents common sense, which is the antithesis of deep spirituality. Again, the soul at such moments is intensely active; self-realization, conscious or unconscious, is the key-note of its state; but Authority expects passivity and obedience. The soul is ready to risk and to dare much if only it may expand; but Authority is bound to lay stress on what is static and safe, and appears to lead to stagnation and sterility. The soul finds that its sheet-anchor is an interior truthfulness, a deliberate, formally willed determination to follow such light as it possesses at all costs; but Authority has to insist upon conformity to an external standard, an orthodoxy, the identification of truth with certain formularies. The soul, at such times, cannot rest short of the conviction that Beauty, Truth, Goodness, Spirit—all the great things of life—are inherent in and energize through the whole of the phenomenal world and the life of

man, however great to the individual may be the cost
of their attainment; but Authority tends to divide the
phenomenal world up into two spheres on the same
level, in one of which Beauty, Truth, and Goodness
are manifested and in the other ugliness and error and
evil, as if all the good in the phenomenal world were 'in
some one particular place or enclosure'. Finally, the
man in such exalted moments with an intensified vision
of the ideal, has an intense realization of the contrast
between that ideal and the low level of his own average
achievement and that of the average achievement of
his fellow-men; but Authority cannot afford to dwell
upon the tragic note or to be anything but optimistic,
at all events as far as its own action and the results of
that action are concerned.

If this diagnosis is true, 'the deadlock,' as von
Hügel says, 'would appear to be complete'; and the
matter is made worse by the modern realization that
in the study of science, of history, of scholarship, of
human nature in general, the inevitable bias of official-
dom has always been more of a hindrance than a help.
Is it true then, as has been asked, that 'a grown man,
or at least an Anglo-Saxon or Teuton, requires no
support or check except those of his own mind and
conscience?' (*Essays*, ii, 11).

Von Hügel's answer is No. What looks at first
like 'an act of manly simplification' is a dangerous
mistake. In spite of the fact that strenuous souls—
that all souls in their strenuous moments—are irritated

by and rebel against officialism, it is an essential factor in the soul's solid growth and balance and in its usefulness to others.

For, first, the Past has its claims: its significance is not exhausted: it is a real element in the Present: it has a right to assert itself; and it is a safeguard against what he calls 'a rude jerk to another level which might upset healthy progress for the many altogether'. Moreover, the average man and the average level of life of each individual man, have also their rights, and need to be protected against the possibility of the ideas of a minority deteriorating into 'a mere trick and fashion, a puerile preciousness, an inverted, doubly base Philistinism'. Again, the average man, and all men in their average moments, need protection against the possible consequences of their own inherent weakness and liability to error, and such protection is afforded by a reference to the standardized experience of other men and to knowledge acquired in the past, and this is what Authority makes available, or claims to make available. The standard of Truth which it holds up may need at times to be revised, but Authority is the recognition of the supremely important fact that objective Truth is independent of individualistic conceptions, and is a safeguard against the possible vagaries of Subjectivism. Further, though Truth, Beauty, and Goodness are everywhere present, it is not true that they are everywhere equally present: in some lives, some institutions, some religions they are, as it were, more concentrated, more completely expressed than in others: they are not evenly distributed, and it is no less unjust to hold that all lives, doctrines, or institutions are equally good and true than to refuse to recognize that there must be some sort and degree of goodness and truth in any man or institution or teaching that manages to keep alive at all. Lastly, the optimism with which Authority regards the *status quo* is not unreasonable; for all hope of a better future must be grounded upon the 'growth, liberation, and concentration of the germinal, imprisoned, scattered good already at work in the present'.

And if officialism of some sort is necessary to protect the many against the danger that the enthusiasm of the few may degenerate into a sort of 'gnostic, esoteric, Palace of Art infatuation', it is no less necessary to provide a continuous means of applying the genuine force and light of the strenuous few to the duller, more automatic many. There must be no monopoly of enlightenment. The interdependence of mankind, at all levels, at all times, and in all races, is indestructible. 'Love,' he says, 'is supreme over knowledge, and Action over speculation.' The corporate spirit alone must rest at the foundation of all man's relations to his fellow-men. 'Any soul large and open enough to hear the heart-beats of the many' will realize 'the essential necessity of Institutionalism for all normal religious education and for the development of even the most interior gifts' (*Essays*, ii, 15).

Thus we get the idea of 'a rhythmic inspiration-

expiration life in the breathing of any living Church'.
It is 'ever and everywhere, both progressive and con-
servative: both reverently free-lance and official; both,
as it were, male and female, creative and reproductive;
both daring to the verge of presumption, and prudent
to the verge of despair'.   At the same time, he is clear
and definite that though official organization and
Authority are necessary means of religious life, they
are means and not ends.   'There is nevertheless a plain
priority of logic and of worth on the side of life.'   The
individual is 'bound to external authority only as to
an instrument, realized by himself as such, for his own
further progress and for his social-religious union with
his fellow-men'.   This is hardly the orthodox view of
the authority of the Christian Church, but he believed
it to be justified by the results of the historical investigation of the circumstances amidst which it had its origin.
The Church, for him, is a body which is 'directly
Christian and Divine only in its germinal and most
elementary features and functions'; and which is
'directly busy with bearing its share in helping on that
ever-growing, ever-renewed experience and embodiment of those sacred realities from which Authority
itself derives all its rights and duties, and of which it is
but the consecrated, ceaseless servant' (*Essays*, ii, 23).

Ten years later von Hügel delivered at Edinburgh
an address on 'Certain Central Needs of Religion, and
the Difficulties of Liberal Movements in Face of the
Needs: as experienced within the Roman Catholic

Church during the last Forty Years' (*Essays*, ii, 91 ff.), in which he dealt with some contemporary manifestations of the Modernist spirit which he regarded as exaggerated or erroneous. The subjects with which he dealt have their denominational aspect, with which we are not here concerned, but he lifts them above the denominational level, and his treatment of them throws useful light on his philosophy of religion.

Thus he discusses the bitter hostility which is often shown against what he calls the sense-symbol-sacrament conception. This hostility he believed to have arisen, not so much from any dislike of the idea itself, as from misconceptions of what is meant and certain practical abuses which have been associated with it. His position is that you cannot get away from the fact that the body and sense element in human nature does play a large part in religion. It is not a matter of the disembodied spirit. It is true that the mind and its intimations and certainties are not, as the Sensualist school of Philosophy maintains, the same as the senses and their impressions, or merely distillations or concentrations of the purely sensible impressions. They are 'something essentially distinct and different' (*Essays*, ii, 99). But it is equally true that they only arise in our minds, 'at least in the first instance and more or less up to the end', as the result of the stimulations experienced by our senses and the impressions conveyed by them, and of our memory of what we have experienced. This, he says, no competent psychologist of the present day would deny: and he refers to the well-known cases of the two deaf-dumb-blind girls, Laura Bridgman and Helen Keller, whose minds were found to be entirely destitute of any idea of God, of the soul, or of their own personality, until means were devised, after endless patient, ingenious investigation, to find substitutes for the sense-impressions which they lacked and through which alone these ideas apparently can be mediated. The artificial process did not produce the ideas but it was a necessary condition of their production. Thus body and soul are bound together into a single human nature: the sacramental principle is as deep as life: and any attempt artificially to dissociate religion from the body-and-sense element, instead of leading to liberty and growth, results in something 'unassimilably thin, abstract, doctrinaire, inhuman, driving men into endless self-occupation and scruples'. The dragon of Subjectivism again rears its head.

CHAPTER VIII

THE belief that it is a metaphysical fact that the spiritual is mediated through the sensible, the eternal through events occurring in the phenomenal world, underlies von Hügel's treatment of the question of the place and value of 'historical facts and contingent institutions' in religion.

Are they necessary? Or supposing that it was discovered that a particular religion had been based upon a belief in the occurrence of events which could not be substantiated, could the religion get on equally well without them? Would it be all the same if they were sublimated into mere symbols of spiritual truths? His answer to this is quite clear. 'There is no such thing,' he says, 'as an exclusively spiritual awakening to, or apprehension of, spiritual Realities' (*Letters*, p. 349). The idea that religion, and in particular that Christianity, can be emancipated, in the supposed interests of safety, from 'the complications and uncertainties of contingency' is 'impossible and ruinous'. All the great religions have had a historical origin; and, in his striking phrase, 'In actual life Natural or Rational Religion or Pure Theism exists as the mirage after the setting, or as the dawn before the rising, of a Historical Religion' (*Essays*, i, xvi). Religion in general is a mere abstraction, and the so-called 'Religion of every honest man,' as we have seen, is 'a sorry stump'.

But it may be urged that historical occurrences belong to the sphere of the contingent: they are established or invalidated by evidence, and the evidence on which they depend is amenable to the same process of critical examination and sifting as any other kind of evidence. Does this mean that, to use the words of Kant, 'the man who is most at home in Greek and Hebrew and the like will drag all the orthodox believers, in spite of all their wry faces, as though they were so many children, whithersoever he may choose'? Was Lessing right when he wrote to Schumann that 'Contingent truths of history can never become the proof for necessary truths of Reason'? (*Essays*, ii, 27). The religious life, it will be admitted, is concerned with the eternal order: can it be satisfied with what happens once for all? Is it not bound up with what is always happening afresh, with the continuous present and not with the past?

This is the question with which he sets himself to deal in the paper on 'The Place and Function of the Historical Element in Religion' read to the London Society for the Study of Religion in 1905. He meets the metaphysical difficulty by first drawing attention to the distinction between the Natural Sciences, which are concerned with the apprehension of Laws, and the

H

Historical Sciences which are concerned with events. 'Reality,' he says, quoting Professor Rickert, 'becomes Nature for us when we contemplate it with reference to the General; it becomes History when we contemplate it with reference to the Particular' (*Essays*, ii, 32). These two aspects of Reality are not mutually exclusive; for the study of History issues in the discovery of laws, and the data of the Natural Sciences have a sort of history: but the subject-matter of History in the ordinary sense is not a mere series of isolated occurrences.   The events with which it deals are not a mere procession of successive incidents.   Human values and ideals are developed and maintained not in Time, but in Duration, and 'History is busy with realities which, at bottom, even here and now, are not in Time at all' (*Essays*, ii, 53).   That is to say, the facts of History are not merely contingent, but are in their very nature vehicles of the expression of a transcendental order.

As for Kant's argument that it would appear to be dangerous in practice to link Religion and History very closely together because that would leave the ordinary man at the mercy of the critical expert, which is the same as Miss Petre's difficulty already referred to, he meets it by an appeal to facts.   Any force which that argument possesses rests at bottom upon a distrust of the powers of the mind of man: it is essentially a sceptical argument.   Now we have seen that von Hügel's whole outlook is positive and optimistic.   However true it may be that the process of arriving at truth involves errors, false starts in one direction, retractations in another, on the whole and taking a broad view, we do reach something substantial and permanent. This can be demonstrated in the case of the other sciences, and it was his opinion that the application of the critical and historical method to the study of religious origins, which, he says, 'has now perhaps achieved maturity, has attained and perfected a whole series of results of the most striking and far-reaching kind' (*Essays*, ii, 28). And he thought that there was no reason to doubt that the newer forms which the study of religion in general has now assumed would in their turn yield contributions to truth of no less permanent and abiding value.

But at the same time, where there is growth there must be growing pains; and it is not surprising if, while the experts are exercising their proper functions of exploration and criticism, the ordinary man is sometimes confused and inclined to ask what is to be the end of it all. This is part of the price which has to be paid for the acquisition of new truth; but it must be remembered that, in times of transition, men are always apt, to use von Hügel's words, to be 'greatly overimpressed as to the range and depth of our real discoveries and final revolutions', and that, if they become 'thus bewildered as to the ultimate facts and laws of the spiritual life', those facts and laws nevertheless 'persist substantially as they were' (*Essays*, i, 222). Wisdom in the end is justified of her children.

But if it be accepted as a principle that a full, concrete religion for practical, everyday use needs a nucleus of assured and critically testable factual happenings, as the soul cannot get on without the body, the application of it to a set of conditions in which the activity of criticism seems to shake ancient beliefs to their foundations is obviously a matter of extreme complexity and delicacy. It is difficult to create, and still more difficult to maintain, amongst more than a picked few, a sufficiently high level of intellectual patience and of faith in the fundamental position—what he calls the major premise —of organized religion (*Essays*, ii, 108).   He draws a distinction between what he calls the major premise, that a nucleus of historical fact is necessary, and the minor premise that it is the business of Authority to maintain, at any cost, the precise formulation and interpretation of belief which has long been accepted. The claim to infallible certainty on every point of detail 'cannot fail, more or less, sooner or later, to find itself in conflict with the historical workers and their conclusions', and to endanger the very principle of a historical nucleus itself.   He is not afraid to face the logical consequences of this admission; but, he says, 'The Creeds would remain true, even if this or that of their articles would have slowly, cautiously, to be reinterpreted as true in not a factual sense or in a factual sense somewhat different from the old one' (p. 109). That Christianity rests upon a basis of ascertained facts is incontestable: if historical criticism proves that it

also developed certain fact-like pictures and symbols of
its belief as well, 'such pictures and symbols are not
necessarily false, though their truth will be not that of
happenedness'.   It is undoubtedly true, as Professor
A. E. Taylor has recently said (*The Faith of a Moralist*,
ii, 41), that 'No historical religion can be sublimated
without remainder into a philosophy, however true and
exalted, without destroying its peculiar character': but
a historical religion may at times have to face the
question whether there are not elements in its tradition
which destroy some of its power of appeal to a modern
mind, or may even be found inconsistent with the
essential spirit of any religion which claims to be
absolute and universal (J. H. Muirhead, in *Hibbert
Journal*, April 1931).

In the Introduction to the *Mystical Element of
Religion* von Hügel says that three great forces have
been at work in Western civilization.   The first is
Hellenism, with its thirst for richness and harmony in
life; the second is Christianity, with its revelation of
personality and depth; the third is Science, the apprehension and conception of brute fact and iron law.
These forces combine to form a deep and complex
whole.   It is the same with Religion.   'If Religion
turned out to be simple,' he says, 'in the sense of being
a monotone, a mere oneness, a whole without parts, it
could not be true' (*Mystical Element*, i, 50).   The great
religions all contain three elements, which he seems to
think may be roughly equated with the three already

mentioned. There is an historical and institutional element, represented by an ancient traditional cultus: an emotional and volitional element, represented in ethical and spiritual experience: and an analytic and speculative element, represented in a philosophy of religion. There is always a tension between these three elements, or it may be that the two first combine against the third; but all three are necessary constituents of any religion worthy of the name. The complete religious man carries within him the dependence on external symbol or authority of the child, the questioning, rationalistic spirit of the youth, and the mystical and emotional feelings and volitions of maturity. The value of a religion depends upon its apprehension of the relations between the three elements and upon the maintenance of these in due proportion.

This is no simple matter; for no individual possesses them in perfect balance. Most often there is a strong bias in one direction or another, and the individual naturally tends to drag religion as a whole over to the side with which he is most in sympathy. This is inevitable, and to a certain extent it is justifiable. The idea of simplification always has an irresistible appeal to the religious mind, and this is intensified in times of transition which bring with them disturbance and confusion. But truth as a whole cannot be lop-sided, and a religion which claims to be absolute and universal cannot be content with anything less than the whole of truth.

When the waters are out, and the country submerged and old landmarks are disappearing it is not surprising if tradition clings desperately and sometimes blindly to the past, and can think of nothing except the immediate necessity of stemming a destructive flood. When old fetters are being loosened, old burdens cast off, old impediments removed, it is not surprising if the sense of recovered freedom sweeps the adventurous speculative intellect on towards a new outlook in which the present seems to be wholly disconnected with the past. And when the battle is joined and the issue still in the balance, it is not surprising if those in whom the mystical, the personal, the subjective side of religion is strongest seek to find a refuge in some sort of transcendentalism which seems to set them above controversies which are concerned with the contingent.

This is the broadest and the most level road, this is the line of least resistance, to concentrate thought and endeavour upon the aspect of truth which has the strongest personal appeal. The individual is urged along it by all the force of his own predilections, and it issues, no doubt, in a conception of religion which seems to present the simplicity and clearness of which he is in quest. And this is, historically, how religion grows. It is the tension between the parts which gives the driving power to the whole. But if there is to be a philosophy of religion, its use and its justification must be found in the fact that it is an endeavour to keep the balance and, as far as may be, to present the truth, the whole truth, and nothing but the truth. It is always easy to over-emphasize or exaggerate, but over-emphasis and exaggeration imply the omission of inconvenient facts. But there must be no omission of facts in the philosophy of religion, and inasmuch as the facts with which it deals are the deepest, most penetrating, most universal of all facts, and the Reality which it seeks to apprehend nothing less than the totality of what is real, it is not to be supposed that any honest attempt to combine them into a system can be anything but a matter which demands the highest intellectual honesty and moral integrity, or that they can be embraced within any simple, easily comprehensible formulas.

Hence for von Hügel the pursuit of religious truth is a long and arduous quest, an endless adventure into the regions of the absolute, which is impeded alike by one-sided insistence upon any one of the three elements to the exclusion of the others, or by the natural yet fatal craving for a greater degree of definiteness and clearness than the subject-matter admits of. The human apprehension of the infinite, however true as far as it goes, must necessarily, he says, 'be varying and in itself obscure. How for man, with all his present physical and psychical limitations and distractions, could it be static and clear?'

'We get to know such realities slowly, laboriously, intermittently, partially; we get to know them, not inevitably nor altogether apart from our dispositions, but only if we are sufficiently awake to care to know them, sufficiently humble to welcome them, and sufficiently generous to pay the price continuously which is strictly necessary if this knowledge and love are not to shrink but to grow.   We indeed get to know realities in proportion as we become worthy to know them, in proportion as we become less self-occupied, less self-centred, more outward-moving, less obstinate and insistent, more gladly lost in the crowd, more rich in giving all we have and especially all we are, our very selves.   And we get to know that we really know these realities by finding our knowedge (dim, difficult, non-transferable though it be) approving itself to us as fruitful; because it leads us to further knowledge of the realities thus known, or of other realities even when these lie apparently quite far away; and all this in a thoroughly living and practical, in a concrete, not abstract, not foretellable, in a quite inexhaustible way' (*Essays*, i, 104).

Let me try to sum up von Hügel's outlook on the great things of life.

He is no purveyor of new religions.   He has nothing to offer as a substitute for God.   At the base of all his thinking, philosophical or religious, there is the foundation of a massive, rational Theism which lies deeper down even than his Christianity.   For him the problem for perplexed spirits in the present day lies not so much in the choice between Theism, Materialism, Pantheism, Pluralism, Agnosticism in any of their forms, as in the reconciliation of the Theistic belief which has been built up in the course of ages and finds its highest and purest expression in Christianity with difficulties which the modern outlook on the world and the ascendancy of the scientific temper have elicited or rendered acute. For him, behind the varying currents of human thought, behind the rough-and-tumble of human activities and sufferings, all good in their way, there stands a Figure, the Centre and Source of all Reality, the ultimate explanation of everything in the phenomenal world. Men have sometimes said that there is no such Figure. Such a position he regarded as beyond the reach of argument. Or they have said that, if there is, it does not much matter because man cannot know anything about Him. Hence his insistence on the need of a critical epistemology. Or they have represented Him as force or energy or some other impersonal abstraction. This is to offer a stone to one who asks for bread. But at the back of it all in the course of the centuries an elevating and purifying process has been at work which has issued in a conception of God which is definitely and demonstrably more exalted and worthier than any which have preceded it. Accretions, the result of loose thinking or loose living, have fallen off of themselves or have been chipped away, and again and again, as the rubbish has disappeared, new aspects, new features of the Supreme Reality have been disclosed.

Long periods have sometimes elapsed when the current idea of God has sufficed in the main for man's intellectual and spiritual needs at the level attained. At other times there has been a disarticulation between his growing aspirations and the ideas which have served their purpose in the past.   But all through the Figure has been there—something objective, something unchanged, something other and greater than man.   Man cannot make a religion; but if he is honest enough, and humble enough, and is willing to pay the cost, he may find one.   All projection of human thought and feeling upon the void and magnifying them indefinitely may lead to an imaginative ideal, but do not lead to religion any more than the *a priori* activity of the intellect leads to a knowledge of Nature.   You cannot impose your own scheme upon Creation, and you cannot impose your own religious philosophy upon God.

Nor is there any need for man to exercise his inventive powers.   His business is to learn.   And the Figure in the background does not stand aloof, but meets human aspirations by a process of Self-revelation, both in the realm of Nature and in the realm of Spirit, both in the experience of the individual soul and in history, which has operated continuously through the ages.   Man cannot at any time comprehend the whole of Truth, but Truth lies before him 'indefinitely apprehensible', and at each stage the standard reached is true so far as it goes.

Isaac Penington, one of the most notable of the seventeenth century Quakers, wrote long ago:

'All truth is a shadow except the last—except the

utmost; yet every truth is true in its kind.   It is a substance in its own place, though it be but a shadow in another place—for it is but a shadow from an intenser substance; and the shadow is a true shadow, as the substance is a true substance.'

A member of the Society of Friends in the twentieth century, and a distinguished man of science, Sir Arthur Eddington, has made use of language which is almost identical.

'If our so-called facts are changing shadows, they are shadows cast by the light of constant truth' (*Science and the Unseen World*, p. 55).

We may be content to leave it at that.

INDEX

MADE AT THE
TEMPLE PRESS
LETCHWORTH

GREAT BRITAIN